IS AMERICA FALLING APART?

What Surprised Me about the United States

MAHNAZ B. CONSOLVER

iUniverse, Inc.
New York Bloomington

Is America Falling Apart?
What Surprised Me about the United States

iUniverse books may be ordered through booksellers or by contacting:

iUniverse
1663 Liberty Drive
Bloomington, IN 47403
www.iuniverse.com
1-800-Authors (1-800-288-4677)

ISBN: 978-1-4502-3268-5 (sc)
ISBN: 978-1-4502-3269-2 (dj)
ISBN: 978-1-4502-3270-8 (ebook)

Library of Congress Control Number: 2010907565

My email:mahnazbc@gmail.com
Blog in English:mahnazbc.blogspot.com
Blog in Farsi:mahnazbc.blogfa.com

Printed in the United States of America

iUniverse rev. date: 06/07/2010

To my wonderful children, and to all the people who live in America, land of opportunities.

INTRODUCTION

In this book I speak my mind about a free country, America. It is what I have seen with my own eyes, what I have heard with my own ears, and what I have felt with my own heart. I point out some of the things going on in this free country that every single person needs to help fix. These problems pose a serious danger to upcoming generations.

My three children and I moved to the United States as Iranian Muslims. We faced a lot of surprises. We also had to make some adjustments to have a better and more comfortable situation and life in America. In this book, you will read about my shocking surprises about dogs in the United States. My life here had a huge impact on how I used to think about them and how I am toward them today.

As a child living in Iran, I heard wonderful things said everywhere about America and Americans. At school the way the teachers sometimes talked made me wonder if America was a country or a perfect dreamland, a fantasy heaven that I could only see in my dreams or read about only inside my beautiful storybooks.

At home when I occasionally heard the news on television, it was all good news about America. I was so obsessed with John F. Kennedy and his family that I wrote a song about him when I was in high school. I still remember most of my song and have done my best to translate it to English.

> *God, what if you brought Kennedy back to life?*
> *He was kind and tender.*
> *He was a kid's dearest friend.*
> *Once I had a friend who is now gone.*
> *It is always night without him.*
> *Even the stars won't shine.*

My heart is blue, my eyes are tearful.
God, if you could bring him back,
Bring him back as a child's best friend.
Bring him back as a shiny star, which can shine again.
He was kind and tender.
His gentleness, sweetness, and rightness made me wonder.

When I grew out of my childhood and became a teenager, my oldest sister got married and moved to America. She never mentioned anything but good about America. I started to wonder, maybe there is a real land of pureness and love on this earth. My sister sometimes mailed or brought me clothes "made in the U.S.A." I wore them everywhere and made sure to tell my friends they were from the land of glory, America.

When I was about fifteen years old and paying more attention to the news about America, I still never heard anything negative about this land of humanity. My positive thoughts grew rapidly about the United States.

One of my friends at school had an older sister who was married to an American man. They still lived in Iran at that time, so my friend had information about Americans too. She often told me her brother-in-law was very easygoing and innocent and did everything right.

I started to think all the people living in America were perfect and did not know the meaning of wrongdoing. I thought that was the reason the United States was a superpower. Americans lived large, and they were all well-educated and in perfect shape. (I never saw a fat American or heard about one anywhere, either on television or in newspapers and magazines.) I was sure all Americans were free of guilt, and they all had a place to live and were well-behaved. No woman dressed up without high heels, and no man dressed without a tie. People exercised and ate smart, women and children were happy, and no child lived in poverty.

I had so many positive thoughts about this magical dreamland. I dreamed that one day I would be able to visit this magic land, and I did. Let me share with you the things that surprised me about America—but let me first tell you that I was especially surprised by the negative things that were going on in America. I had never suspected there would be anything negative in the United States.

In this land, there shouldn't be any poor, homeless, or hungry people. There should be no abuse of women. There should not be other negative things, because of the opportunities America offers to its people and the people who come from all over the world. Outsiders come to this land to take advantage of the powerful and beautiful opportunities, yet some Americans are in deep sleep. They don't even care or see or feel what a great country they are living in. Because of their lack of knowledge, this country is going downhill very quickly.

The purpose of writing this book was to wake some Americans up from their deep sleep and get them involved in doing their share to help solve the problems that are a huge threat to this land of glory today. This book is good for anybody, especially parents and single people.

WHAT SURPRISED ME ABOUT THE UNITED STATES? THE AIRPORT

As soon as the plane landed at John F. Kennedy International Airport in New York, I honestly thought I had landed on another planet. I became so confused and even dizzy because so many things caught my attention at once. The airport was humongous, and it had a very shiny and clean floor. There were people in beautiful and colorful clothes, different kinds of people from all over the world in one place. There were all kinds of food and restaurants and many different kinds of stores. People were very well-dressed and walked quickly, with their heads up and their shoulders straight.

I was shocked and deeply involved in my observations—this did look like my magical dreamland, I thought. The second thing that caught my attention strongly was when I went to use the bathroom.

THE BATHROOMS

Let me first tell you about the bathrooms that I used for almost eighteen years before I came to the United States. The bathrooms in Iran come in different shapes and sizes, some very fancy and some simple, but the toilet is a hole dug in the ground that you sit on in a squat position very low to the ground; that is how you do your business. In some houses there are also toilet seats just like here; we call them toilet farangie in Iran.

As a matter of fact, we did have a toilet farangie in my dad's house, but the door to that bathroom was always locked unless we had guests over—it was only for guests' use. I never used that toilet farangie while I was living at home. There were also two Iranian-style bathrooms in my dad's house: one was inside the building and one outside in the yard.

In emergency cases, such as if we were sick or if it were night, we were allowed to use the one inside the building; other than that, we were supposed to use the one in the yard. My dad was very sensitive to the smell, and I think that was the reason for him to also build one in the yard. As long as my dad wasn't home, I used the inside bathroom. By the time he was home, it was dark and I had an excuse not to go to the yard bathroom. I never liked the outside bathroom, and it was not as fancy as the one that was inside.

Anyway, as soon as I stepped in the airport bathroom, I was shocked and forgot why I was there. The good smell, the huge mirrors, the brightness, the cleanliness, and the size of the bathroom amazed me. The other thing that caught my attention was that nobody was looking at me. For a moment I thought I was invisible and they did not see me; but when I paid closer attention, I realized they weren't looking at each other either.

I was amazed and stood in a corner and stared at the women. Some were fixing their hair, some were redoing their makeup, and some were washing their hands and refreshing themselves. For a while I just stood there and observed the ladies coming and going out of the bathroom. Believe me, every single move they made was surprising to me.

Women were doing personal things in the bathroom in front of each other like nobody was watching them. Everything they were doing was normal to them but not to me; all the things they were doing I had learned that I need to do in private—such as farting, putting makeup on, raising their skirts in order to fix their stockings, and blowing their noses. When I noticed a lady reach under her breasts and raise them a little to be in a better and higher position, I was so put to shame that I placed my hands on my face to cover my eyes and pretended I did not see her. But I kept peeking at her through the open spaces of my fingers.

I did not even know how to use the hand blower to dry my hands or, in some bathrooms, how to get the paper towels out of their place. I had to learn everything about the bathrooms in the United States.

PEOPLE SMILE AT EACH OTHER

The most pleasant experience was that people greet one another, even though they do not know each other. I still can recall the beautiful smiley face of the woman who said hi to me thirty years ago when for the first time I came to the United States. *How did she know me?* I asked myself.

I realized that wonderful people light up their faces and also the faces of others with beautiful smiles. I realized American people have an easy but more effective language to communicate in, the language of love (*smile*), and that is how they grow their love to a greater level for their family, friends, and each other.

I learned from these people that a happy face is free therapy for me and the others around me. It costs nothing, yet it speaks out from somebody's beautiful and warm heart. Americans know they do not need to express their love, care, and kindness to others by words—their smiles and actions say it all.

THEY ARGUE BUT ARE STILL FRIENDS

I was pleasantly surprised when I witnessed people in America sometimes argue very harshly, but at the end, they shake hands and remain friends. As time went on, I noticed they do not attack each other in the argument; instead, they attack and argue each other's idea. That was a sweet and exciting experience for me.

The more years I lived in the United States, the more I became familiar with life in America.

THE WAY AMERICANS DRIVE

It was a nice surprise to see most drivers following driving laws. I was amazed at the police power in America, which has a huge impact on the way people drive. But another reason is the people themselves paying attention and obeying the driving laws. There were times I witnessed the traffic lights were out of order, but people were their own police and followed the rules step-by-step with no police around—those moments were very pleasant and sweet for me.

On the other hand, there were also unpleasant moments of driving in America. I am completely against drivers who dial numbers and talk on their cell phones while driving. I became even sadder when I realized some people text while driving. Driving and texting increase the chance of a crash twenty-six times over. People who are texting while driving routinely take their eyes off the road for five seconds. A lot might happen during these five seconds.

I believe texting and driving is at least as bad as drunk driving—it might even be worse. I always believed that to drive safely, we need to fully engage our brains and attention to the road and other innocent drivers. I become very worried when I see a teenage girl riding a bike and talking on the cell phone. Are we honestly so short of time that we need to do lots of other things behind the wheel and put our lives and the lives of others in danger?

I noticed that people often do other things while driving. I have seen many set their dogs on their laps, facing the steering wheel. What if the dog's legs get stuck in the wheel? Some eat and drink while they are driving. Some get deeply involved and engage in conversation with others in the car. Some get distracted by their kids. I have even seen some yell and scream at their kids. Some dance with the music in their car, and some play very loud music that won't let them hear the siren of an ambulance or a fire truck that is approaching. I have seen people kiss each other while driving. I have seen some change the CD or tape in their car while driving. Well, for your information, you can do all these things before you start the car. This might well save some lives.

On the other hand, getting a driver's license is very easy for teenagers. The driving age in the United States really surprised me. Having such a low driving age leads some teenagers to use the car as a toy and a source of fun, while they put their lives and the lives of others in danger. I believe the driving age should be higher. Also, more practice hours should be required, and more responsibility should be demanded of teenagers. All people must feel a hundred percent responsible when they get behind those wheels.

DRINKING AND DRIVING

What is the difference between somebody killing a person out on the streets or in a bar versus a person who drives drunk and kills somebody? The bar or street killer goes to jail for maybe forty years or more, but the drunk driver who kills somebody usually does not go to jail. Even if he or she does go to jail, it is usually for a very short time.

The second difference is that the first killer put one person's life in danger, but a drunk driver put his own life and the lives of many innocent people and children in danger. If you were the judge, which one deserves more punishment? I am not a lawmaker, but somewhere something does not make sense about the drinking and driving laws. Isn't the priority of government supposed to be the safety of the community?

I was not sad to find out about the huge numbers of drunk drivers—I was mad. News reports stated that one hundred fifty-nine thousand innocent lives had been taken in the last decade due to selfish drunk drivers. Fifteen hundred died in California alone in 2008. Think about it for a moment: fifteen hundred got killed just because selfish, irresponsible drunks chose not to call a cab or a friend when they were drunk. Shameful, isn't it? These fifteen hundred innocent people were somebody's father or mother, they were somebody's sister or brother, they were somebody's daughter or son, they were somebody's best friend—so your selfish drunk driver not only killed those fifteen hundred innocent people but also destroyed their families. What a shame!

Three in ten Americans drive with alcohol in their blood, according to news reports. Is the criminal justice system failing to enforce the laws against drunk drivers? The average person that is convicted of DUI has already been driving under the influence of alcohol eighty-seven times before getting arrested for DUI Guess what. If the law is not harsh enough against drunk drivers, the same driver will put people's lives in danger eighty-seven more times before he or she gets the second DUI What a huge risk the lawmakers are taking, risking innocent people's lives.

Even though I am an outsider and not familiar with the laws, I know enough to say something is wrong with the laws about driving drunk. If the law was harsh enough, it would stop or decrease this crime. We need more aggressive laws to get the attention of drunk drivers and get them off the streets for good.

Let's do something about it and save the lives of innocent citizens of great America. Do not treat a drunk driver as a sick person. They are not sick. Their act is evil, and they should be considered as criminals. How can someone put people's lives in danger and not be considered a criminal?

Let me have a straight talk with you, selfish alcoholic. You have given up your life, your reputation, your dignity, your honesty, your family, your mind, your body, your friends, and your future just to be out of this world for a while. Just because you are weak and can't face your problems, just because in your thoughts this is the only way to solve your problems!

Let me tell you, this is just a big problem adding to the small ones you already have. Be a real human being and act like a real one; step up and fix your biggest problem. When you are abusing your money and your own body, how can you care about others? Protecting yourself and others requires good decisions. How can you make honest decisions when you use alcohol or drugs? You are nothing but a selfish criminal!

CHILDREN WORK HARD, BUT SOME HAVE NO KNOWLEDGE OF HOW TO SPEND THEIR MONEY

Do not buy it if you don't need it, don't buy a new one if the old one is still usable, and don't buy an expensive one when you can search for a lower-priced one. Teach these lessons to your children. Make sure they have control of their money in a smart way; they must not let the items have control of their hard-earned money. Teach them to think before they spend. Do they really need the item, or do they just want it? These are the important steps we need to teach our kids from an early age.

I was very happy and surprised to see lots of work opportunities for teenagers available in restaurants, gas stations, shopping malls, sports centers, grocery stores, and other places. There are fantastic opportunities for teens to work in this country. Such opportunity doesn't exist in most other countries. But do teens honestly know how to spend their hard-earned money?

Working generally keeps kids away from trouble, but if they don't know how to spend their money, this money might lead them to trouble. I have seen many teenagers work very hard for their money, but they often don't appreciate the value of the honest money they make, and some spend it on drugs.

I did research at work for many years to see if the boys are smarter about spending and saving their money or the girls. I concluded girls are smarter about their money. I have seen some teen boys make their money in difficult ways, but then spend it against themselves, against their health and minds to buy and use drugs. They are so young; some do not even know these dangerous little pills they are buying with their honest pennies can take so much away from them.

They do not know these drugs can cost them their lives, their families, their hard-earned money, their reputation, their friends, and a lot more. It is so sad to see some teens in America work so hard and spend so unwisely. We as parents need to teach them from an early age how to save and spend their money wisely by giving them weekly money and keeping track of it, making sure to reward them when they are good with their saving and spending.

I remember I was not good with spending my weekly money and keeping the money in a piggy bank. My mom came up with another idea. She became my bank and kept my money. She even made her own checks and gave them to me; whenever I needed money, I would write a check and withdraw money from my mom's bank. She even made me write on the corner of the check what the purpose was of writing that check. At the beginning, she kept track of my spending: Why? How? Where? These were the questions that I couldn't leave without answering.

My mom's idea was so fun; it was like playing a game. That fun little game had a huge impact on my financial life for years to come. After a while I was on my own, and I still kept track of my money very well. We as parents are the key for everything; that's the purpose of parents—to teach our children the best possible way to fly.

It's easier to educate our children about saving and spending their money when they are very young—much easier than what they go through later in life, always being in debt. Have love, time, and respect for your children. Kids are great. We as parents need to be great to raise them better. Teach your children to be respectful toward their money and love their body. If they respect their money and love their body, they won't spend their hard-earned money on drugs.

WASTING TOO MUCH

This is a blessed land, very beautiful, very green with lots of rain most of the time, altogether a very blessed and beautiful country. Americans are blessed in many ways, but this doesn't mean they should waste in many ways. Don't forget there is an end to everything that exists except God. No matter how blessed you are, if you spend and waste more than you need to, you will be broke sooner or later.

This is one of the saddest experiences I had in America. Some people in this blessed land waste too much—and worse than that, their children are becoming just like them. Some are food wasters, some are money wasters, and some are time wasters. It's never too late to learn and teach. If you as a parent don't know things in life, learn! That's the only way lives get better and easier for you, for your children, and for the next generation to come.

Every day I try to learn something new about life. That keeps me alert, sharp, and happy. I am also able to deal with problems more easily and tell others how to deal with life too. We are here on this earth, aren't we? We all need to survive in this world, don't we? We don't just live for ourselves; we live for other people and for future generations. Alexander Graham Bell invented the telephone, but he could never make a phone call to his family because his wife and daughter were both deaf. He lived to help future generations. Every little help in any way possible that we can provide for the future counts, doesn't it?

Do not waste, please. Do not waste God's blessings; instead, appreciate his gifts. Does not waste water, do not waste food, and do not waste electricity. Do not waste gas, clothes, school supplies, time, or anything else.

Remember: There are always people out there who can use your waste. Your trash may be somebody else's treasure.

What follows is reality. Please read it carefully and with attention. You can find these statistics all over the Internet by searching for statistics about water supplies.

A child dies from a water-related disease every fifteen seconds.

The emerging worldwide water shortage is very serious.

It's been said we are going to run out of water before we run out of oil.

The groundwater in several countries is almost gone.

A shortage of water leads to shortage of food and much higher prices.

Our water problem is fast becoming a hunger problem.

It's time to give water a second thought.

One toilet flush uses three gallons of water.

A single load of laundry uses forty gallons of water.

A ten-minute shower uses fifty gallons of water.

Of all the water on the earth, only three percent is fresh water—and most of it is ice.

A water crisis is looming.

In the twentieth century, the world population tripled, yet the use of water grew six times over.

By the middle of the twenty-first century, there will be an additional three billion people. Most are born in countries already experiencing water shortages.

By the year 2020, the population is expected to reach twenty-two billion.

Millions of people in the world already live on less than three gallons of water every day, and one in five doesn't have access to safe drinking water.

The average American uses about one hundred sixty gallons of water every day.

I had no idea we would have such bad shortages of water in the near future. After I researched water to write about it in this book, I became more aware of this crisis. The more you get educated and learn, the more you know what to do, and life gets easier for you and others.

Nowadays I have reduced my use of water by almost half. I know now that every drop counts. I do it for myself, for my children, for others, for the country, for the whole world, and for the next generation. Don't use the dishwasher unless there is a completely full load in it. Don't stay in the shower with the water running the whole time. If you have several dishes in the sink to wash, don't let the water run the whole time. Don't let the water run while you brush your teeth or shave.

It would make a big difference if every single person participated in not wasting water or other things. You can do a lot to prevent wasting water. If you see somebody wasting water, it's all right to tell them why they should not waste water. The reason they do it is lack of knowledge; but when you give them your knowledge, they will often be happy not to waste it anymore.

I thought people in America would celebrate Thanksgiving by thanking God for his blessings and by not wasting those blessings. Unfortunately I was wrong. In many cases, I was present at wasteful Thanksgiving parties. Is this the way God wants us to thank him—by buying too much, cooking a lot, preparing more than we need and, in the end, wasting too much?

I was sadly surprised that meaningful holidays have lost the real meanings—now it's all about eating, gifts, and wasting. I believe not wasting is a free therapy for our own happiness. You can buy and cook less and give the extra money away for the hungry and homeless children in the United States or all over the world.

I was shocked at how people can eat that much on holidays, especially Thanksgiving; they eat much more than they are capable of. When I asked somebody how he could eat that much on Thanksgiving, he thought that was a funny question; and he told me, "Thanksgiving is all about eating."

My grandma used to say, "Quit eating before your stomach is full." She said, "Eating too much makes you feel like a drunken person and you are not able to think clearly." She also mentioned that a waster doesn't have a good reputation in the eyes of God. So ever since I was a little girl, I have never overloaded myself with food.

When I saw one of the employees at McDonald's who was doing the dishes and placed only two dishes in the dishwasher, I approached her quickly and opened the dishwasher door and asked her not to run the dishwasher unless it had a full load in it. She got upset and asked me, "Why do you care? You don't pay the bills here, do you?" I said no, I didn't, and then I took time to explain to her nicely why. I gave her my knowledge, and I never saw her wasting water, electricity, or gas at work again.

When we went to a Chinese all-you-can-eat restaurant and witnessed people and their children grab too much food and at the end leave most of it for the trash, it really bothered me. The food sitting on the buffet is God's blessing to us; we are not supposed to waste it.

Believe me, it only takes two minutes to educate your child in a place like this. ("Sweetheart, grab a little. Then if you are still hungry, food is on the buffet for you the whole time we are here. You can always get more.") Try it and follow up on it; kids do listen. This way God will like you more, the restaurant owner will appreciate it, you will feel better about yourself, and most importantly, your children will learn not to waste. You can spend two minutes to educate them and save thousands of dollars of their money in the future. Isn't it worth it?

The bad thing is that some people think only about themselves. That's not right! We need to think about ourselves, our family, our friends and people in need, our country, other countries, our planet, and the next generation. Then we won't be wasteful.

We need to educate ourselves and our children about upcoming shortages of water, food, gas, and other things—this is the only way we will get serious and quit wasting. Children love to feel important—don't take that away from them. Educate them and ask for their help. Let them feel great.

When I turn off the water or the light that I am not using, I am not only saving on my bills. I also feel like I am making a constructive move to save our planet. Isn't this the easiest way to help and feel wonderful about having an impact in this world? This is a free therapy to bring peace to you, make yourself happy, and make yourself feel important—try it.

During my fifteen years of living in the United States, I have seen it all. I have seen people spend out of control. I have seen people spend money that they don't even have. I have seen people cook more than they need and throw God's blessings in the trash. I have seen how customers and restaurants waste much. They don't just waste food—they waste anything. Yet in the same country of America, I have seen homeless women and children in need of a good meal. My grandma used to say that if you waste too much, you will end up in poverty.

I have seen some people who have full closets of nice warm clothes—yet in the same country, homeless little boys and girls are in need of a warm coat in the winter. Helping a needy child can give you incredible satisfaction. I have seen furniture with no use in a garage or basement of some people's houses— but a single mom with children, no matter how hard she works to provide and at the same time to take care of her kids, she is not able to do so.

If you have a place to sleep, a roof over your head, clothes in your closet, and food in your icebox, you are richer than some people who don't. Instead of wasting, share. You can't make a trash can happy and smiley by giving it your waste, but you sure can bring a beautiful smile to a hungry child's face by sharing. Even a single dollar can go a long way and make your heart happy.

Isn't sharing a beautiful thing? Isn't share a beautiful word? So isn't it better, instead of wasting much, to share with the little homeless children? Use less; save and share more.

BABIES HAVING BABIES

According to the Guttmacher Institute, seven hundred fifty thousand teens in the United States get pregnant every year—what a disaster. I was sadly amazed by the number of children having children or children trying to raise children. These children are having babies before they are mature enough even to handle themselves. Remember, we don't only raise babies; we should raise adults, fathers, moms, husbands and wives, sisters and brothers. How we raise children has a huge impact on their future and adult years. The saddest part is a lot of these pregnant children don't even know who the fathers of their babies are—that was a shocking surprise for me.

Why don't parents teach and educate their little girls about the realities of life and having a baby when they are not ready? Eventually you are the one who's going to get burned if you don't educate your little girl, because you are the one who is going to end up raising the child most of the time. Believe me, I have seen lots of children that don't know who and where their mom is and that have been raised by their grandparents.

Why not remind your little girl not to have a baby since she is a child herself? Why not remind her that babies are not pets and toys? Why not teach our little girls the huge responsibilities of having babies? These young moms, or I should say little girls, obviously don't have the ability to make right choices because if they could, they wouldn't get pregnant in the first place. How can they raise a child without knowing anything about children? Forty percent of babies in the United States are born out of wedlock, according to research I found on the Internet. Isn't this a disaster? Most of the children that come from one-parent families struggle.

We can't look at babies as pets, even though a responsible person will give his or her pet love, time, and care. Some even take them to training classes and educate them so they behave responsibly. Sadly, some parents don't even give their children the time needed to raise them responsibly.

What does a little girl know about getting or not getting pregnant? They don't know anything; that's why they do it. You as parents are the key to educating them and solving this problem. A huge amount of this disaster is the parents' fault for not getting involved and educating their little girls. Be realistic—having and raising a baby is hard work. Please recommend your children to practice safe sex.

GETTING HELP FROM THE GOVERNMENT FOR NO REASON

First, let me tell you I am absolutely not against government help for the sick, disabled, single parents with insufficient income, and people who have lost their jobs. The reason I had to add this to my book is that I have seen very healthy people get help from the government for no reason; their only reason is they don't want to work. I am absolutely against such laws.

I have seen people get help from the government just because they are lazy. I do not think the government should reward those who do not want to work and punish the ones who work proudly with dignity. I do not think taxpayer money should go to people who simply do not want to work.

I was shocked when I found out that some people get food stamps from the government and then sell them. An employee one day told me he had no food in his refrigerator. I asked why. He said he spent all his money on other things.

I was in the process of finding a way to help him until I saw him at work the next day. He had a smile on his face. I realized he was not worried anymore, so I approached him and asked, "Do you still have a refrigerator with no food in it?"

He said, "No, I bought somebody's food stamps."

"Didn't that person need the food stamps herself?"

"I guess not," he said.

"If they didn't need them, why did they get them?"

He said, "To sell them and get cash for them."

In another case, one of the employees quit work. After several days, she came back with a piece of paper in her hand and asked if I could sign it so she could get help from the government. This employee was single, with no children, very healthy, and very young. The first thing I asked her was why. She said she needed to survive.

"Is something wrong with you or are you having children?" I asked.

"No," she said.

I said, "I am so against healthy and able people getting a free ride off others." I refused to sign the paper for her. Instead, I told her that on every street, there are restaurants with signs on their windows about hiring people. "Go get a real job instead of begging," I told her.

I have seen other similar cases. If there are so many free riders around me, there must be a lot more all over the United States. It is very sad how some people cheat the government and waste taxpayer money in different ways.

The law should be very harsh on people who request help from the government. I just can't believe how easy the government can be cheated in the United States.

I believe getting free money from the government for no specific reason has a lot of downsides for the government, taxpayers, and especially for the healthy and able who are searching for a free ride. I think when the young and healthy don't work, they get in trouble and crime much more than the ones who do work.

The ones who don't work even if they aren't sick become sick, depressed, obese, and confused. They also feel lonely, tired, bored, and hopeless—all signs of being useless and not working. Working and being active make you healthy, sociable, and happy and keeps you away from evildoing. Besides all that, you feel proud, and this good feeling leads you to other positive activities when you make your own money.

When you don't work and get a free ride, you feel in your heart like you are nobody. Most of the depressed feeling comes from feeling useless. You don't have to feel that way—get a real job and feel proud.

MEDIA, TELEVISION, COMPUTERS, AND GAMES

As two adventurous friends were passing by elephants, they suddenly stopped, confused by the fact that these huge creatures were being held by only a rope tied to their legs. It was obvious that the elephant could at any time break away from the rope that they were tied to, but for some reason they didn't. One friend saw a trainer nearby and asked why these magnificent animals just stood there and made no attempt to get away.

"Well," said the trainer, "when they are very young and much smaller, we use the same size rope to tie them. At that age it's enough to hold them. As they grow up, they are conditioned to believe they cannot break away. They believe the rope can still hold them, so they never try to break their old habit and go free."

The two friends were amazed. These animals could at any time break free from their bonds, but because they believed they couldn't, they were stuck right where they were. The powerful and gigantic creatures had limited their present abilities by the limitations of their past.

That's what we are doing to our children today; we are wrapping their thoughts only around TV, computers, games, and cell phones. We are limiting their young minds to games and computers. That's the only lifestyle they are experiencing; it's called a mind-set.

If you are addicted to drugs and alcohol, that's a mind-set; that's the only lifestyle you know. If you are a woman-beater, that's a mind-set; that's the only lifestyle you know. If you have lots of debt on your shoulders, that's a mind-set and the only lifestyle you know.

If we let our children get addicted to their cell phones, games, computers, and television, we are encouraging them to have their mind-set only around these subjects. It's very dangerous, with no good result most of the time.

You can always break free of negative mind-sets or thoughts and replace them with positive ones, but only if you want to. You can always replace the bad choices with good ones. It's all up to you.

Let's talk about the role of media in America. I was sadly surprised to see that American teenagers' role models mostly are the ones who show more skin, do more drugs, and do more crazy things to get the attention of the younger generation. Surprisingly, the media is helping them.

When Britney Spears, today's young generation's role model, flashed the most private part of her body while she was getting out of the car, for several days, not only did the regular channels keep showing and talking about what she did, but also all the news channels did the same thing. Honestly, didn't they have anything more important to show, talk about, or teach the young than Britney Spears's wild behavior? Do the media have to make sure every single young person in America hears about her ugly move? What about the ones who have their mind-set around Britney Spears and copy every move she makes?

What about Lindsay Lohan's drug use or Paris Hilton's sex tape that kept going on TV and the Internet for a long time? Wasn't there anything wonderful going on in America at that time to replace the ugly news about these three people? Weren't there any geniuses, inventors, musicians, athletes, or do-gooders at schools to talk about instead? Are we rewarding the bad and punishing the good?

Do our children do anything besides go to school to chase each other— boys after girls and girls after boys—use drugs and search on the computer, talk on their cell phones, watch TV, and play games? What do they see or hear everywhere they turn? Why do you think most teens are out of control these days? Why do you think a huge number of them use drugs? Why do you think Britney Spears comes at the top of the list of most-searched-for people on the computer? It's because most of the young look at her as a role model. I am sure she must do well for society too. Why not talk about the good things she does and make our kids follow her footsteps in a positive way?

The number of young getting out of control is increasing rapidly because they can't find a decent, good role model on TV or the Internet in America. I can honestly say about 90 percent of shows on TV are trashy (I am talking about the ones made for teenagers and the young). Unfortunately the media is not doing a good job for teenagers and the future of America. I am very sure there are a huge number of intelligent, athletic, inventive children who live in America. Why don't we hear about them that much? Instead, they are usually called nerds and made fun of at schools. There are times the creativity dies in them just because they don't get the encouragement that the trashy ones get.

Teenagers are the future of America; the media should play a positive and educational role for them. There is not going to be a better future for America if the teens of this country go downhill this quickly. Let's give the love, attention, and care to the real role models, the ones who really deserve it.

Why do you think a lot of the young want to be like Britney Spears or Lindsay Lohan? It's because the media give them too much power and attention. That's how our children learn from them and want to be like them; our children think if they follow their footsteps, they can be famous like them someday. The young are not knowledgeable of the facts in life, so whatever the media dump in their fresh brains, they catch and use it—but at what cost? Give attention to the real role models that have been ignored for so long. We as parents are the key. It's all up to us how we train and teach our children.

There are some evil people who live in our communities. Arsonists set fire to the forests or to innocent people's houses, sometimes with the people trapped inside. The media give them more satisfaction by showing the fire time and time again. If an evil or sick-minded person kills a bunch of people, he is rewarded by being on TV and having a movie made about him or a book written about him. What better reward does he want? His evil act is going to encourage other evildoers to do the same. This way other sick-minded or evil people are encouraged to try to do better in crime and get ahead of other evildoers. That's one of the reasons these evil acts won't stop and the evildoers keep coming up with something new every day.

I am a human being like you. I have emotions like you. I get happy, upset, and angry. I relax by watching TV. I cry, get inspired, get encouraged, get disappointed, feel guilty, get loud by watching TV and listening to the media. I learn from watching TV; I get educated, get motivated, and get inspired by listening and watching the media. Through the media I find out about the people who are capable of doing well for others because I only search for the good in the media. But believe me, there are some inexperienced, innocent young people who get confused and sometimes make bad choices from what they see in the media. There are also sick-minded people who get their inspiration from the media.

The media need to get more involved with positivity for the sake of the young in America. Who are the next generation? Everywhere I look, mostly I see alcoholics, drug users, losers, and the depressed—are these the future of America? If they are, there is not going to be a good future for America. Those with sharp brains—not alcoholics and drug users—make a country move ahead.

Everything has become a business in America. We should not look at everything as a business, especially when it comes to our children, especially when America is going downhill so fast that every single person needs to wake up and look around with wide-open eyes and start doing his/her share of helping.

Parents say they don't have time for their kids. The kids are growing up by themselves, and then the kids turn to the media, TV, and the Internet. What is a child-molester looking for? A lonely child!

What do our children see and learn from the media? What TV shows dump in your kids' brains, they learn—and it's mostly trash. Please, for the future of America, we all need to do something about it. One or two hands don't make much noise, but a lot of hands make a loud noise and do better. We need the parents' help, the teachers' help, the magazines' help, the media's help, and everybody else's help to fix these problems.

I know you are aware of all these scary problems. If there is a person who doesn't see any problem in this country today, I say that's because that person is a big problem himself or herself. Why keep criticizing and not do anything to fix the problems? Instead of doing something, why do we dump our problems on each other's shoulders and at the end expect government to do something for us? Government is not in our house to see how much we care for our kids or how we raise them; government is not in our house to see how irresponsibly and carelessly we raise our children sometimes.

When we see a problem of our kids or others, we as parents need to step up and fix it. It's time for every single person living in this country to roll up our sleeves and start helping in any way possible. Otherwise it will be too late.

Is the media doing the job they should for our children and the future of America? Isn't there anything more important to show on TV than sex, killing, fire, and drugs? When it comes to TV, almost all the shows for the young are trashy. What do you think the younger generation takes away from shows like that? Are shows like that going to help them or hurt them? You be the judge. These days there are a lot of these shows on TV. What are they thinking? Do you feel safe as parents to leave your teens at home alone with the TV and the computer? Do the media and the Internet make life a living hell for parents?

The media is poisoning the mind of the young, and nobody seems to care. What about you people? What about you responsible parents, and what about you unknown real role models? Do you care? If you do, you need to take it into your own hands and do something about it.

Let's encourage our children from an early age to get engaged with good books instead of wasting hours of their lives in negativity in front of the television, the Internet, and games. We need to teach them good books are their best friends, best advisers, best trainers, and best teachers. They need to know a good book doesn't poison their beautiful mind, doesn't disappoint them, doesn't let them down, doesn't depress them, doesn't encourage them to use drugs and alcohol, and doesn't make them commit suicide. A good book is our and our children's best friend and can save them from falling. A good book can also teach us how to live a better life. Bring up your children with a habit of book reading. Doing good is starting to disappear among the younger generation in this country, and the media has a huge role in it.

Not long ago I was invited to a party. All the adults were gathered upstairs, and the children and young from age five to twenty-five were gathered downstairs. I always like to be among the children as well as the adults. The children's behavior always interests me; I like to observe the cute and innocent way they act and talk. Besides, I learn a lot from them, and they make me feel young, fresh, pure, innocent, energetic, and happy. So I spent most of my time downstairs with the children and adult kids. My friend found me among the kids and said loudly, "The oldest child downstairs is forty-eight years old." Funny, but I felt fourteen among the kids.

The whole time I was with the kids, they were playing games like they never had a chance to play before in their lives. They were playing with love and passion, not wasting a single second. The older ones were more aggressive toward the games and took over very quickly; and the younger ones, who were kind of ignored by the older kids, had brought their own games and happily started to play. Nobody had time to talk, to eat, or to enjoy each other's company.

Their moms brought full dishes of food and placed them everywhere because obviously they didn't have time to eat. This is sad. Think about it for a moment: children and adult kids are wasting their lives by using too many computers, games, and cell phones. Games have complete control of our children's lives and brains (mind-set).We need to develop smarter ways to make them stay away from this danger. Besides, these games kill the other talents in our children by limiting their thoughts. Also, children can't find time to find out who they really are and what they really are capable of. It seems children these days don't live in a real world.

Anyway, at the end of the party when I looked at every single kid, they looked tired and stressed. They didn't know what they had eaten; they weren't even aware they were there to spent time with each other, not the games. Their hundred percent focus was on games. How sad!

Then I was reminded of my own childhood. Whenever there was a party going on, kids were running and playing hide-and-seek, ping-pong, soccer, badminton, and other games. We played real games. We also laughed, told jokes, danced, sang, created new ways to have fun, rested, giggled a lot, and relaxed in nature. Sometimes older kids looked at my dad's books and borrowed books from him to read. When it was time to eat, everybody from the youngest to the oldest got together, ate happily with huge enjoyment, and then every single person was thankful for God's blessings. That was the good old days. These days we do not let our children be children anymore.

If we as parents don't know how our kids can entertain themselves, we need to educate ourselves first. I realize some parents try to make the kids leave them alone by giving them wrong tools, not aware of the violent role some games play in our children's minds and lives. Sometimes kids ask and beg for these new toys, and parents provide them without thinking. Educate yourself about all the things that are available to your children that will help them grow up. Try it. Make a little change, and see a big result.

Why do you think some of the shootings at schools take place? Where do you think the shooters get their inspiration from? After playing a gunman in a game over and over and over, their minds get set on the gunman in the game and that's all they see: themselves as the gunman. That's how they have been training their mind. That's the way they have been training their brain, and it becomes the only lifestyle they know.

A child's thoughts can easily change after playing a dangerous character in a game; his/her brain can get entangled with the game. There are healthy and fun games out there. Why not buy them instead? Every time I see somebody with problems, I recommend they watch Oprah and Dr. Phil on television. These two shows give you great knowledge of everything.

Our children often refuse to attempt something new and challenging because of their so-called mind-set. Let's help the next generation move forward in a powerful direction. Leaving the kids on their own most of the time and expecting them to raise themselves is wrong. Children need love, care, time, attention, and guidance; otherwise there won't be many engineers, scientists, honest hard workers, and inventors in the future of America. Raise your kids for the future, able to face the problems and the facts and realities of life.

The hours our children spend in front of the television, on the phone, and playing games add up quickly. Statistics can be found all over the Internet.

Today's twenty-one-year-old has watched twenty thousand hours of television.

Today's twenty-one-year-old has played ten thousand hours of video games and has talked on the phone for ten thousand hours.

More than 70 percent of America's four-year-olds have used computers.

Today's twenty-one-year-old has sent two hundred fifty thousand e-mails.

Our children might be the greatest at anything, but these days they do not have time to try it. They need to try different things besides games, cell phones, the Internet, and TV to find out who they really are and what their capabilities are. Technology is great, but there should be limits for everything. *Good luck!*

SCHOOL AND PROBLEMS

I always thought school meant a safe, educational, and secure place for children. When I started to send my children to school in the United States, I felt relaxed and confident that they were in good hands and safe places. But as time went on, my dreams and thoughts about schools in the United States changed. I could write an entire book about my shocking surprises about schools in America, but let me just put in a few details.

The first surprising thing was that the educational level is so low at schools in America. When my children came from Iran and were placed at the same level they were in Iran, it was very boring for them to work with the class because they already knew most of the things the teacher was teaching. They kept telling me, "Mom, we already have studied all this before." It was then I became aware how low the educational level is in America. I had such a hard time sending three bored boys to school every day.

One of my sons said the first time the teacher entered the classroom, he stood up for the teacher to show his respect—but he realized nobody else did. He said he realized how comfortable the relationship between the teachers and students is in the United States. In Iran when a teacher enters a classroom, all the students rise to show their respect. My kids had to face lots of changes to adjust to schools in the United States.

I had heard that U.S. students didn't have to wear school uniforms, and I kind of liked the idea. But the first time that I made a trip to a high school in the United States, I was amazed at the way children dressed up for the school, especially the girls. I felt I was anywhere else but school. *Is this a high school or a fashion salon?* I asked myself. I couldn't believe my eyes. I couldn't keep my eyes off the way the girls were dressed. I stood in a corner the whole time. I didn't even want to blink; I was so afraid I would miss something.

When I passed two students kissing in the middle of the hallway, I started to blink because I thought something was wrong with my eyes. They were all over each other and way too affectionate for an educational place. I unintentionally stared as I approached them. The students kissing and my staring at them kept going on until I noticed several other students were watching too. I felt a kind of relief that it wasn't only me staring. But when I paid closer attention, I realized the other students were staring at me, not the kissers. *They were the ones who were kissing; I was just looking. Why were the other students looking at me instead of them?* I asked myself. *What a different world,* I thought. *Is this a school or a matchmaking place?*

Then I saw a young male student hand in hand with a female. Both were wearing huge black pants, very wide from the top to the bottom, and weird black shirts with black wide wristbands. They both had very black hair with weird hairdos, especially the male. He had the sides of his head completely shaved, and in the middle the hair was long but somehow standing up in the air. When I paid closer attention to their faces, it kind of scared me away for a minute because they had heavy black eyeliner. The jewelry that was planted by the sides of their noses and on each side of their lower lips gave me a chill.

I always thought freedom was good, but even freedom needs limitations. Freedom doesn't mean the ability to do whatever you want to do. Freedom for constructive performance is wonderful, but freedom that hurts education and respectable places like schools is more hurtful than helpful.

I stood there and thought, *If all the students had school uniforms, the school would look more like an educational place—not a scary fashion salon or a huge Halloween party.*

Boys get distracted by girls' stylish and sexy ways of dressing up. I believe it would make a huge difference if all the students were equal in what they wear at school. A lot of problems would be solved if all the students wore the same uniforms at school. It would draw the students' attention, focus, and time more to their educational matters. Let's make the books, sports, music, and art their main focus, not the trashy clothes. The students need to know school is a place to get educated, get ahead, and be somebody valuable for themselves, their family, their country, and the world in the future.

Unfortunately things are exactly the opposite now. These days most of the students see the school as a place for fashion, romance, drugs, and violent and disrespectful behavior toward teachers and each other. The smart and nice students are being pushed aside and made fun of. They are called nerds by a bunch of jealous, mean, lazy kids. These nerd kids represent the best of America's schools, they represent America's educational place in the world, and they represent the future of America. Why are they the ones who stay unknown and get hurt?

Having two or three choices of uniforms has so much benefit for the students, for the schools, for the parents at home, for the community, and for the future of America. First, the students would not spend much of their money, time, and thought on what and how to wear and show off at school. Instead, they would have more time to pay more attention to their schoolwork, books, teachers, and education. Right now at schools, fashion, drugs, romance, and bullying come first for a lot of students. The students are confused and don't know what their priority should be at school. They spend huge amounts of time to get ahead of each other at fashion or have more girlfriends, boyfriends, or drugs.

There must be some rules and guidance for the students to be more aware of the real reason they go to school. Some don't even know why they go to school, and some have been drawn into their messy worlds and have forgotten what school is really about.

I became a worried mom when I heard my son talking about drug use on break time by some of the students at school. This news went beyond distress in my mind, and I had a hard time believing it. I had to see it with my own eyes to believe it. One day around break time, I went to my son's high school to experience this ugly situation with my own eyes. (My ex-husband used to smoke some kinds of drugs, so I was very familiar with the smell, especially of marijuana and opium.)

I quickly noticed a bunch of students were gathered sitting on the grass under a big tree. I became so suspicious of that group, I took my cell phone out of my bag and pretended I was talking on the phone. I approached in their direction little by little. I had my dark sunglasses on and my head was directed somewhere else, but my eyes were directed toward them.

As I got closer, I realized they were passing something around. When I got a little closer, I could smell the weed they were smoking. They all got up and went different directions after they saw me close by. I was so disappointed that I felt a pain in my heart. I sat on the grass and laid my back to the same tree where the students were a little while ago.

My son was right. *But what was the solution, what if my children started doing that?* I wondered. Before that, I had always thought my kids were in good hands at school and always felt relaxed when my kids were at school. All of that changed at that very moment.

I cried. I begged God to protect them and asked God if he could have my kids in his own hands. I prayed for the students who were smoking just a little while ago. I remember I prayed a lot that day. I don't remember how long, but I just know I spent a long time under that tree, frightened and confused. I also couldn't feel any energy in me. That was the most disappointing surprise of all time living in America.

Are the principals, school advisors, parents, and school lawmakers unaware about what's going on at schools and what's happening to the future of this country? If I could find out that easily about students smoking weed at school, everybody else could too. Not everybody has money for private schools, which are more secure. What about the public schools that most of the kids go to? Have we forgotten about the public schools? There should be more discipline in public schools, with the parents' help. Children are more hurt in schools these days than helped. We as parents need to do our share of helping toward the awakening and education of our kids.

Teens are teens. Most of the times they don't know, we as parents need to educate them. Maybe as parents we don't know either. Every problem has a way to solve it. We can educate ourselves first; it's never too late to learn and then teach our children. Teens and kids are smart. When they see their parents making changes for a better and healthier lifestyle, they will gladly follow their footsteps.

The only time we find out how much we don't know is when we learn. Most of the things we do to hurt ourselves and our family are because we don't know. Why do you think kids use drugs? In some cases they see their parents do it. In some cases they don't know what drugs do to their minds and bodies, so they don't say no to the drugs. In many cases, they don't know how to say no to a drug-addict friend.

Let me tell you a story about a seventeen-year-old teenager who worked with me. His name was Amin. He had lost his father in a car accident when he was only nine years old. I realized that almost all the teens a little older or younger than he smoked at work, but not him. After a year of working with Amin, I was completely sure he did not do any kind of drugs at all. One day I told him how proud I was of him not smoking any kind of drugs and cigarettes. Then I asked him what his secret was.

He said that when he was a little boy, his dad kept making him aware of the damage of drugs and even showed him a film about drug addicts and how their lives were going to end. Amin said that film did it and made him aware of drugs' damages. He said looking at the drug users in that film scared him away from drugs for the rest of his life. Amin's father spent maybe several hours to educate his son about drugs but saved his son's lifetime—how wonderful! Isn't that worth it? The earlier we start to educate our children, the better result we get.

If the children are not getting educated at home, why not educate them at school? Why shouldn't teachers at the elementary schools go beyond teaching subjects and find a little time to teach children how to live better lives? Sometimes the teachers can go beyond teaching the subject and make the students aware of the realities in life.

It would be a life-changing matter for the students to become familiar with the facts of life. Some could even educate their parents if they needed to. I don't see anything wrong with the kids parenting their parents, but the teachers need to educate the students in an entertaining way because when the students have fun, they learn better. The danger of drugs is attacking our children, families, schools, communities, and country. Why not do something powerful about it and save millions of lives?

As I said, there is a solution for every problem. We just need to set our goals, have a plan, follow up, and get everybody involved to fix this killer problem. We as parents are the key, and we must be responsible to work together with our kids and schools to solve these problems. Remember: what you put into your body is what you become; it doesn't matter if it's unhealthy food, drugs, negative thoughts, and alcohol or nutritious food, positive thoughts, love, and self-esteem.

News reports tell us that 65 percent of kids at schools are bullied. There is lots of bullying going on in American schools, including both verbal and mental abuse. The schools need to be more harsh and persistent in their anti-bullying policies. Some kids even commit suicide as a result of being bullied by the mean students.

I think the bad students get jealous of the good ones and use bullying as a weapon to give the good students a hard time. You as parents need to help your innocent children who are being bullied. You need to keep reminding them that the only way to win against bullies is to stay focused, get more educated, and get ahead in sports, music, art, or any other field at school. My dad used to say, "The only way to torture your enemy is to do good in life and stay healthy."

Unfortunately, the school zone in America has become a danger to, or a war zone for, our children. Some parents don't even dare to send their kids to school, so they homeschool their children. I know some of these parents. When I asked why they homeschool their children, they all had the same answer: the schools are not safe, and our kids learn a lot of bad things there.

I believe the smart and nice students get bothered and punished by groups of mean and jealous students just because they are smart and do well at school. The weird thing is some of the nice students join the bad groups just because they are weak, scared, and want to be protected; so they end up with a bad choice. Respect or disrespect starts from the family. If we disrespect our kids, they go out and do it to others. Be respectful toward your children and teach them how to love, care, and share in their lives. They need to know that when they are good, good comes to them. A good person is always a winner, and a bad one is always a loser.

I was very surprised to see some pregnant teens at school. I thought that was the result of that kissing or at least that was how it started. The high school that I was witnessing looked like anything but an educational place. It was certainly not a safe, healthy, and secure place for children in America. We should focus a hundred percent on what works the best for our children at schools.

I noticed they gave away very unhealthy food at schools, a kind of food just to fill up the students' stomachs, not do anything for their brains. The kind of food that makes them tired, sleepy, heavy, and lazy. The unhealthy snack machines and unhealthy drink machines make it even worse. Can't they spend the same amount of money on healthy food for the students instead of unhealthy? Give the students healthy choices and make it a good habit for them; give them more brain food than stomach food. In this way they will stay in shape, stay focused, and get more energetic.

When I look back at the time I was going to school, the government had a plan giving away breakfast at school because they believed breakfast was the most important meal of the day. They also believed some students didn't have the habit of eating breakfast and this caused them to fall behind in their studies. Around nine in the morning, they gave breakfast to all the students in the classroom right in front of the teacher, and the teacher made sure that everybody ate their breakfast. The breakfast mostly included boiled eggs, toast, milk, big healthy cookies, bananas, apples, cheese, and walnuts, which are the most common breakfast items in Iran.

After fifteen minutes the class would go back to normal, with better energy and as happier students. The students' brains functioned better, and they learned better. Remember, what you put in your body and mind is what you become. The food at schools in the United States sucks. Where do you think part of the obesity comes from? It comes right from the schools. Educate the students how to eat healthy at school. Isn't the reason children go to school is to get educated?

I get worried observing lots of obese children at schools these days. They are just victims of lack of knowledge; they don't go to the store to buy food for themselves. What they eat is what you as parents and the schools feed them. They are honestly just little innocent victims; pay more real attention to them.

My mind was blown away when I heard some teachers sleep with their minor students in middle schools and high schools. Is the teacher supposed to be a role model or a sex machine? If you as a teacher are a respectful trainer, you belong to a respectful place, namely a school. But if you are after people's teens, you belong in jail—it's your choice.

My son told me he answered a difficult question in the classroom and received a thumbs-up from the teacher, which made him mad and confused. In Iran thumbs-up has the same meaning as raising the middle finger in

America. When he found out that in America thumbs-up means well done, he said he was still confused but not mad. This was one of the funniest surprises to us. I wouldn't do a thumbs-up to anybody, even my American friends, for a long time because in my mind, it didn't have a good meaning.

When your kids go to school, make sure you have direct control of your kids choosing friends. They need to know that those who surround them influence what they will become and accomplish. Choose relationships carefully. An enemy is anyone who destroys our children's dreams for their future. Remember, the less dead weight the kids carry on their shoulders, the higher they are able to fly. You can't fix or control what's beyond repair. You can't fix the unfixable, so let's fix the problems while they are still small and fixable, before it's too late.

Moving in a right direction is more important than moving fast. Spend more time with your kids and show them the right direction. Teach your children to be strong. The real victory of life is jumping from one failure to another, growing and getting stronger, without losing trust and hope before achieving their dreams.

Kids need to know wrong is wrong, no matter how hard they argue to make it look right. Why don't we make our children familiar with very beneficial good books? This way from an early age, our children learn how to manage and deal with stress.

We have not gotten anywhere by the ways currently practiced at schools. Let's make some changes in schools and try some new ways. I think the school buildings are big and beautiful, the technology they have at schools is beautiful, the libraries are big and beautiful, the sports equipment is beautiful, but what is going on inside the schools is not beautiful.

I believe teacher quality is much more important than anything else. Most of the teachers are heroes. They work so hard for so little. The least we as parents can do for them is to teach our children to show respect and listen to them.

TEEN DRUG USE IN AMERICA

Did you know nine hundred thousand teens sell drugs in the United States? That means nine hundred thousand little young lives are in danger, and your teen might be one of them. Your life is made of your choices, and what makes your life worth living is good choices. Teens and young people think death is only for old people and they will never die; but if you show them videos of teen drug use and death, they will believe death is not only for old people but also for young drug users.

Teach your children a real recognition of the importance of choosing a real friend. Teach them that a very dangerous person most of the time wears a very friendly and nice smile to be able to get his or her victim. They need to know not to trust anybody before that person is known by the family. Even adults can fall into these evildoers' nets. All of Bernie Madoff's victims were yesterday's teens. There are a lot of Madoffs out there living among innocent people. There are also lots of drug dealers and drug users who are trying to get your innocent children into their nets.

I was shocked when I found out the biggest drug market in the world is the United States—the perfect country of my childhood! I was more shocked about the teens' drug use. When I saw a two- or three-year-old child smoking weed on TV, I became both angry and sad.

What makes the drug market so successful is the demand for drugs. Teens see the use of drugs as a part of growing up and being somebody. They often think it's cool and that they are doing what a normal teen is supposed to do. Some just simply don't know how to say *no* to their drug-user friends. They aren't aware of the consequences that go with drug use.

I have said some *yes*'s in my life that haunted me for a long time until I was able to fix them. Children should be taught to say *no*. I know that when you are a teen, saying *no* is hard, but we as parents need to train our children's thoughts toward the *no* word. *No* is a beautiful word if they learn when and how to use it from an early age.

This beautiful word *no* protects your kids or even you from harm from drug users, from drug dealers, from bad doing, from evil friends, from alcohol, and from harmful pills that are pouring in from doctor's prescriptions, drug dealers, and the Internet. Can we control all of these? Of course not, but what we can do is to train our children the best way possible to deal with all these threats. I learned the best and easiest way to say *no* to others is to say *no* to myself first. If you can teach your children to say *no* to themselves in a dangerous situation, like saying *no* to themselves for the first smoke, the first drink of alcohol, cheating, stealing, and other negative things, it would make life easier for them. In this way we shape their confidence in a strong and powerful direction.

Have control over their relationships with others and make sure they don't get involved in a toxic relationship. A bad friend is capable of anything. A bad friend can lead your kid's life toward danger. Always check their friends' backgrounds, and if they aren't any good, get rid of them very quickly before it's too late. The teen's brain is very fresh and can attract things very quickly without giving it a second thought. That's why you need to be there for them to guide them to the right direction. Honestly, what's more important than spending your time to give your children life lessons and to engage in their lives? How to live a good life is a talent. I have even seen very highly educated people drown in messy lifestyles. They are highly educated but don't know how to live healthy lives. You probably know people like that too.

I have seen kids get involved with drugs and alcohol at an early age. It then stays with them, and they can't get away from their addiction later in life. That's the only lifestyle they have experienced. They need to break the pattern and start trying positive things. A lot of young American students when they party, they party to kill themselves, not to enjoy and have fun. That's why some young American students die during spring break week or when they turn twenty-one and drink twenty-one shots to celebrate. They don't know they are celebrating their death. On a medical news show I watched on July 22, 2009, there was a couple whose twenty-one-year-old son was a great student and athlete. On his twenty-first birthday, he overdosed on alcohol and his brain stopped functioning.

There are too many cases like this going on in this country every day. The solution is to educate our kids. We can't fix the unfixable, and we can't turn back the clock and remember that a party should be fun, not deadly. Drugs and alcohol make your brain ill, and you end up living your life with a damaged brain. Alcohol and drugs just disconnect you from the realities of life for that moment only. Don't let alcohol and drugs control you; don't let your drug-addict friends have control of your life. What about you? Don't you have a brain to use and think smart? Control your body, honor your body, and control your destiny. How can somebody who is abusive to his or her own body and money be caring and loving toward others? You can turn your life around any moment and start living again; anybody can change and do better. Just do it!

EASY ACCESS TO GUNS

I was amazed how many criminals and irresponsible people have guns and how the law makes it so easy for people to get guns. Irresponsible people wouldn't be able to get guns if the laws were harsh enough against them. As we see on the news sometimes, children have easy access to their irresponsible parents' weapons, resulting in their hurting themselves or others. A lot of people get killed every year due to criminals having guns.

I believe guns should only get into the hands of responsible and thoughtful people. They are the only people who do not use guns badly. They also place guns in a safe place so nobody else can have access to them.

Newscasts have reported that America has the world's highest firearm homicide rate. There are more than eleven thousand five hundred homicides by guns every year. Safety in the community should be number one.

IS ANYTHING MADE IN THE USA?

I started to search everywhere when one of my close family members who lives in Iran asked for a made-in-the-USA coat. Before that, I had never paid attention to where my clothes were from as long as they were cute.

My husband and I started to look around. We didn't lose hope for the first three or four stores that we looked at, but slowly after that, disappointment started setting in. The more we looked around, the less result we got. My husband and I were shockingly surprised.

I was determined to look at all the stores in my city to find a coat made in the United States. We found two made in Canada in Van-Mour. After I had checked all the stores, I started to think maybe I had missed something. I checked some of the stores again, but there were no coats made in the United States—unbelievable!

I felt frustrated. I came home and looked at my clothes in the closet. When I found a dress made in the United States, I got so excited and screamed *wow*. I had found one! I even went through my husband's closet, but almost all of his clothes were made in China.

As a result, we bought the made-in-Canada coat. I called my family member in Iran and told him I couldn't find any coats made in the United States, but I bought one made in Canada. He thought it was funny and said, "You might double-check to see if you live in America or in China."

After ten years of staying in America, five years ago I finally decided to make a trip to Iran. I bought lots of good, expensive gifts for family and friends from the stores in America. At that time I still wasn't aware that there is very little merchandise made in the United States available in the stores. Almost all the gifts I bought were made in China. Instead of making everybody happy, I made them mad, and they acted like I let them down.

"Did you come from China?" a friend asked.

"Do you live in a Chinatown?" another friend asked.

"There is plenty of merchandise in Iran that was made in China. If we had wanted to buy something made in China, we could buy it here in Iran. We wanted something made in the United States," somebody else said.

I had no idea people in Iran were that obsessed with merchandise made in the United States—or were so sensitive about where their gifts were from. I always thought that when we gift somebody, we gift from the heart. The thought of gifting and thinking of someone is what's valuable.

Several months later, we decided to buy a new clock for our living room. I told my husband, "Let's buy a made-in-the-USA one." We started the search, and very soon we found out there is no such thing as a made-in-the-USA clock.

People all over the world search for products made in the United States, which are reputed to have the highest quality level; yet stores in America are all full of products made in other countries, especially China.

Is anything made in the United States anymore? Read the following statistics reported on FOX news.

Ninety-five percent of clothing sold in the United States was made in the United States in 1965.

Eighty percent of such clothing was made in the United States in 1975.

Fifty percent was made in the United States in1990.

Only 5 percent was made in the United States in 2009.

Perhaps we need to see more merchandise made in the United States being sold in the United States.

AMERICA, LAND OF DIVERSITY

One of the most wonderful things about America is its ethnic diversity. I never felt like a stranger in the United States. In 1979 when for the first time I took a walk around the University of Houston, I realized how mixed the people in the United States are. I saw Asian, American, Indian, Iranian, and all other races all gathered in one place. I was very impressed.

I was more amazed when for the first time I went to the Galleria Mall in Houston and witnessed people from Mexico, Japan, Australia, Iran, Cuba, Africa, Taiwan, and China. People from all over the world live together as one community, but with different cultures and traditions. This shows the generosity of American people, and it is one of the things that make America great and different. During all these years, I have learned so much about other countries by meeting a lot of different people from different countries.

The United States has inspired and captured the attention of people of other countries for its values, freedom, human rights, women's rights, and opportunities. People from all over the world move to the United States to pursue happiness and freedom and get the best chance of opportunities. I have been blessed to live in America and achieve the rights and freedom that every single woman deserves according to God's word.

HOMELESSNESS IN AMERICA

This just doesn't make sense to me: one in fifty American children experience homelessness in America. Sad, isn't it? About 40 percent of America's homeless are women and their children. Women and their children have been the fastest growing group of homeless for most of the 1990s, according to a 2009 study by the National Center on Family Homelessness.

This was one of the most surprising things for me to believe. Why is there such a thing as homelessness in this world of opportunities in the most powerful country in the world? This crisis also threatens public safety. No child should experience being homeless. Children are pure, innocent, and hopeful; they change our lives for the better; they give us a reason to live; they give us a better understanding of what real life is about; they inspire us; and they give us hope, energy, and strength. In return, let's do something for them. Let's have love, care, and respect for them; let's make life a little sweeter and easier for them.

Homelessness has a huge impact on the children who attend school. They are not able to develop a good relationship with other students and teachers, so they can't build self-confidence and strong working habits. I experienced something very shocking when I was working at McDonald's, and it made me think maybe some American people like to be homeless.

One day as the day was dropping into the night, a smelly, unshaved, thin, dirty male, who was wearing a long dirty coat with some holes in it, carrying a big bag on his back and another in his hands, entered the restaurant. He got everybody's attention as soon as he came in. "He is a homeless man," an employee whispered in my ear. I had not seen a homeless person before. Very quickly I asked if he was harmless. The employee told me yes.

He approached me and asked for free food, saying he had not eaten for the last thirty hours. I felt bad for him and gave him a cheeseburger, a drink, and some fries. As he was grabbing the food, I watched him very closely. He seemed very healthy, kind of skinny, about forty years old, and very dirty. He headed for the door after he was done eating. "Sir," I hollered at him. He turned to me and waited for me to say something.

I asked him if he needed a job so he could make and spend his own money and never starve to death or beg for food again. "No" was the answer that came out of his mouth. He drank the rest of his drink, dropped the cup in the trash can, and left. That guy left me with a huge question mark in my mind. *Maybe he enjoys being homeless, maybe he wants to be homeless,* I thought.

It is an absolute disgrace for children to experience homelessness in any part of the world. Children need to experience childhood. They need to be children. They need to experience giggling, playing, dancing, laughing loud, and having fun. If someone's childhood is completely taken away from him or her, they will have a difficult time facing the problems in their adult life. They will ride an emotional roller coaster in the future.

THE ABUSE OF WOMEN IN AMERICA

It is written in the Hebrew Talmud, the book where all of the sayings and preachings of rabbis are preserved for all time: "Be very careful if you make a woman cry, because God counts her tears. The woman comes out of a man's rib. Not from his feet to be walked on. Not from his head to be superior, but from the side to be equal, under the arm to be protected, and next to the heart to be loved."

The most shocking surprise of all—which happened to be the most prevalent one too—was the abuse of women in the land of women's rights.

"Love does not hurt. If a man hits you once, he will hit you again," as Oprah stated March 10, 2009.

Isn't this unbelievable—the abuse of women in the land of equality and justice and rights for women! Why don't women use their rights in the United States?

It honestly freaks me out, especially when I heard on the Oprah Winfrey Show that one in three women in the United States experiences abuse. That's a lot. Opportunities for women mean power, but for some reason women don't see and use good opportunities. Sometimes I think maybe the American women who are abused need to go to countries where there is no such a thing as women's rights. Maybe then they would realize and appreciate what they have and how lucky they are. Maybe because they have it all, they don't appreciate it. We often don't appreciate what we have unless we lose it.

I have my hands. I write, clean, put food in my mouth, cook, brush my teeth, type, work, give away, feed my family, take a shower, make tea, dust—you name it, I do it all with my hands. I never thank my hands, I never think about them, I never appreciate them—but as soon as I lose them, I will find out how important they were and what a big role they were playing in my life.

We have good rains every year, but most people don't care, see, or feel the beautiful crystal drops of the rain and the beauty of nature after each rain. I have even heard some people say, "Damn, it's raining again." But if we didn't have rain for a year or two, the same people would realize the important role of the rain; they would get worried and even say rain prayers.

Why don't we see, feel, or care about the blessing we have and get the best use of it? Women's rights are an enormous blessing for women who live in America. Why not use these blessings at the time of need? By not using their rights at a time of need, women encourage their abusers to take more control and do it to others too. One of the main reasons you are abused is that you let your abuser do so. You as a woman need to put a stop to your abuser's wild acts when you can. There is absolutely no excuse for a woman who lives in America to be abused by her man—*none*, because women have it all. The only excuse for a woman to be abused is that she likes to be abused. Otherwise by a good plan, set your goals and follow up step-by-step, and you can achieve a normal life.

A winner always has a plan, and a loser always has an excuse. A winner always responds to every problem, and a loser finds a problem for every answer. A winner says, "Let's do it," but a loser says, "Somebody do it for me." A winner says, "It may be hard to do, but it's possible." But a loser says, "It's impossible, it's so hard to do." Which one would you rather be? Think hard, then pick.

Teach your children from an early age to have love, care, and respect for themselves.

One of the reasons women around the world let themselves be abused is that they don't know what their real value is; they don't know what they are worth. They don't know how to care and love for themselves. If a woman lets a man abuse her, it shows how she feels about herself.

One day when I was checking my e-mails, I found this beautiful note. I loved it and kept it for a long time. I keep rereading it to make sure to remind myself that I have value. I want to share it with you, friend.

When God created woman, he was working late on the sixth day. An angel came by and said, "Why spend so much time on that one?"

And the Lord answered, "Have you seen all the specifications I have to meet to shape her? She must be washable, but not made of plastic; have more than two hundred moving parts, which all must be replaceable; and she must function on all kinds of food. She must be able to embrace several kids at the same time, give a hug that can heal anything from a bruised knee to a broken heart, and she must do all these things with only two hands."

The angel was impressed and responded, "Just two hands? Impossible. And this is the standard model? Too much work for one day ... wait until tomorrow and then complete her."

"I will not," said the Lord. "I am so close to completing this creature, which will be the favorite of my heart. She cures herself when sick, and she can work eighteen hours a day."

The angel came nearer and touched the woman. "But you have made her so soft, Lord."

"She is soft," said the Lord. "But I have also made her strong. You can't imagine what she can endure and overcome."

"Can she think?" the angel asked.

The Lord answered, "Not only she can think, but also she can reason and negotiate."

The angel touched the woman's cheek. "Lord, it seems this creature is leaking! You have put too many burdens on her."

"She isn't leaking—it's a tear," the Lord corrected the angel.

"What's it for?" asked the angel.

The Lord said, "Tears are her way of expressing grief, her doubts, her love, her loneliness, her suffering, and her pride."

This made a big impression on the angel. "Lord, you are a genius, you thought of everything. The woman is indeed marvelous."

"Indeed she is! Woman has strengths that amaze man. She can handle trouble and carry heavy burdens. She holds happiness, love, and sympathy. She smiles when feeling like screaming. She sings when she feels like crying, cries when she is happy, and laughs when she is afraid. She fights for what she believes in and stands up against injustice. She

does not take no for an answer when she can see a better solution. She gives herself so her family can thrive. She takes her friend to the doctor if she is afraid. Her love is unconditional. She cries when her kids are victorious. She is happy when her family and friends do well. She is glad when she hears of a birth or a wedding. Her heart is broken when a next of kin or friend dies. But she finds the strength to get on with life. She knows that a kiss and a hug can heal a broken heart. There is only one thing wrong with her. SHE FORGETS WHAT SHE IS WORTH."

Sometimes you need to remind yourself how valuable and powerful you are as a woman and what great value you have. Sometimes you need to reward yourself generously for all the things you do as a woman.

Surprisingly 80 to 90 percent of abused women go back to their abuser, according to the Oprah Winfrey Show. I call that addiction love, and it's very dangerous. It has been claimed that on average, three women are killed by their husbands or boyfriends every single day in the United States. If you are staying in a toxic relationship, there is a chance you will be the next one. Sometimes it is better not to have a spouse than to have a toxic one. Don't stay with an abusing spouse. If you do, not only do you destroy yourself, but you also damage your children's childhood and their future.

To the men who abuse their women, try being nice and caring to your woman and family, then see the result. Read the following poem (I found it in my e-mails one day and thought it worth adding to my book).

Whatever you give a woman, she will make it greater.
If you give a woman a sperm, she'll give you a baby.
If you give her a house, she'll give you a home.
If you give her groceries, she'll give you a meal.
If you give her a smile, she'll give you her heart.
She multiplies and enlarges what is given to her.
So, if you give her any crap, be ready to receive a ton of sh—

Oprah reached out to men who used to be woman abusers. It was their first step to recovery when those men broke their silence for the first time. The first constructive and important step toward fixing a problem is to admit to it. I was very impressed with the men stepping out; I believe it takes a real man to do so, a man who wants to do well but doesn't know how.

THE ABUSE OF MEN IN AMERICA

When I heard on the Oprah Winfrey Show that 15 to 16 percent of men in the United States are abused by their women, my mouth stayed wide open for a long time. I had never seen or heard such a thing in my whole life. That was the weirdest surprise of all. I just can't imagine how a man can be abused by a woman, but that's just as wrong as a woman being abused by her man.

If you are a female or male abuser, you can be a real human being and start helping to fix this problem that is out of control. Most problems we have in life, it's because we don't have the necessary knowledge. The more we educate ourselves, the better and faster problems go away. Fear kills the confidence in you. Don't let fear overcome you or have a place in you, because it will hold you back. Always be careful and prepared, not fearful. Always prepare for the worst but hope for the best.

The most difficult step to fix this problem is to make the first move. Remember, we can't fight problems by ourselves; ask for help and guidance. There are plenty of kind people out there who can help you or at least tell you what to do.

That's how I ended up in a women's shelter for the first time thirty years ago. I made some mistakes, but it was a great life experience. Don't we learn from our mistakes and grow from our failures? Once in a while, remind yourself you are there for you and don't let you be forgotten by you.

HOW FAR AN AMERICAN WOMAN WENT FOR LOVE

Some women fall in love on the Internet and have the courage to go for it, no matter how far away their Internet lover lives.

My oldest son, Bob, and I witnessed something unbelievable when five years ago we made a trip to Iran. On the way to Amsterdam, there was an American lady sitting next to Bob in the plane. She was very nice. She was also a talker. Bob was sitting between me and her, but I still could hear her because she was kind of loud for being inside an airplane. She was talking to Bob about how her first marriage didn't work out. She mentioned that she was abused by the first husband.

She was kind of cute, average in weight and height, with long curly blond hair and blue eyes. She was wearing light makeup and was very excited and smiley. She said she had met someone on the Internet and was going to meet him. I became curious and jumped in, asking, "Where does he live?"

"He is from Iraq and lives in Karkok." She kept talking about how disrespectful her first husband had been toward her and how happy she was about finally finding someone who loved and respected her deeply. She really amazed me because not very many women have that kind of courage.

It was lunchtime, so I got a chance to speak to my son. "She must be very brave. At this time of war, everybody is trying to escape from the war zone, but she is going there to meet a boyfriend," I said to Bob. Bob was just as amazed as I was, but he kept quiet, maybe because he was sitting next to her. On the other hand, he doesn't like to interfere in other people's lives. I could read the big question mark in his eyes. The lady had said enough to get me interested in hearing more of her life story.

As soon as I started to ask the lady some more questions, Bob got up and asked me to switch seats. I was glad that I ended up sitting next to the lady.

50

She kept telling me about her previous husband, not knowing that I was more interested in the new boyfriend.

After a long conversation, I found out she had met her new man through the Internet about eight months earlier, and he had invited her to go to Iraq since he wasn't able to come to the United States. I could see the sparkle and happiness in her eyes and feel it in her voice. *At this time of war, I wouldn't even think about going to Iraq, even if I was the loneliest woman and Prince Charming from Iraq asked me to go there,* I thought. I asked her if she felt safe going to a country at war.

She said, "There is nothing going on where my boyfriend lives, and it's safe."

"How do you trust this guy?" I asked.

"I feel in my heart that he is a good man," she said.

I gave her credit for her courage. I wished her the best and said a prayer for her. At the Amsterdam airport, we went our separate ways. Bob and I took the next flight to Iran, and she did to Iraq. "As soon as she gets there and sees the situation, she will turn around and go back to the United States immediately," I said to Bob.

I made some other friends on the next flight and told them about the American lady in love with the Iraqi gentleman. They hardly believed me. We stayed in Iran for a month, and I told all my family about the American lady going to Iraq for love. They all had the same reaction I'd had.

Finally the day came to go back to the United States. We took the flight to Amsterdam, and from there we were supposed to take a flight to America. I noticed my son's eyes were frozen on something while we were waiting to pass the security in the Amsterdam airport.

I followed his eyes, and what I saw gave me an electric shock. I wish someone had a camera and had taken our picture at that moment.

We saw a lady who looked like the American-in-love lady. Bob and I both looked at each other and asked the same question at the same time, "Is that the same lady who was going to Iraq?" Then we both turned our heads toward the lady and started to stare at her again. This time she saw us, smiled, and waved her hand.

"It's her," I said to Bob. "I needed to ask her a hundred questions," I told Bob and approached her very quickly. The reason we were so surprised was because this time she was wearing a long uniform and a big scarf so that none of her hair appeared. She wasn't wearing any makeup.

As soon as I got to her, I asked, "What happened? Did you like Iraq? Did you like him? How was the war? Why are you dressed up differently? Was he a good person?" I just bombarded her with my questions.

She seemed very happy. She said she didn't feel like there was a war going on in Iraq and she loved it there. As soon as she said she got married to the Iraqi Muslim man and she became a Muslim too, my eyes and mouth went wide open and I realized why she was dressed differently.

"Why are you going back to the United States then?" I asked her.

She said her husband didn't want to move to the United States. Instead, she was going back to America and sell everything, then move to Iraq with her wonderful husband and new family.

This time we were in the same plane but different seats and far away from each other, which was a break for Bob. I had to let her go. I wished the best for her, and we went our separate ways. I admired her courage and prayed for her from the bottom of my heart.

This incident opened my eyes. There are abusive men here in the United States. There are abusive men in Iraq too. There are good men here and there. She couldn't find one here, but she found one there. There are some women who can't find one there, but they find one here. That is what women are searching for, an honest and good man. They will give up anything to find true and faithful love. To most of them, it doesn't matter at what price or where. All they are searching for is a loving, caring partner to walk this long road beside them.

Isn't America a country of freedom, opportunities, and justice? She didn't care; she gave up all these for a man who was great in heart. All she cared about was finding a true love. She gave up her family, country, friends, and religion for a true love. That's how much a woman gives up for true love. That's how far a woman goes for a real love.

THE WAY SOME AMERICANS EAT

My grandma used to say, "When you eat, concentrate on what you are eating—the smell, the taste, and the food. Try to taste every single ingredient in your food. Enjoy and think about the taste of onion, garlic, meat, basil, turmeric, the rice, and all the other things you have in your food. What's the use of eating when you think and talk and do other things besides eating? Enjoy and eat God's blessing with no rush and with love."

She always insisted we quit eating before we were full. She said, "If you eat more than you are supposed to, you won't be able to think straight and clearly." (I have to ask Dr. Oz about that.) She always said, "Eat breakfast like a king, lunch like a prince, and dinner like a beggar."

She was invited to our house one day when my brother and I were arguing over something while we were eating. She said, "If you want to stay healthy, don't eat when you are upset. Make sure you have a beautiful smile on, and if you want to talk while eating, talk about funny and beautiful things." She was so sensitive about talking with a full mouth too. (Who isn't?)

"Smile, laugh, and think of beautiful things and God's blessings while you eat," she always taught me. Being happy while eating food plays a huge role in your health.

I realize some Americans don't know what they are eating. I have seen lots of people eat while driving. How can you enjoy and feel the taste of food while driving? I have seen people eat while reading a book. How can you eat and read a book and concentrate on both reading and eating at the same time? It's impossible.

I have seen lots of people eat in a rush. These people don't even know what they are putting in their mouths. I have seen lots of people eat while they are reading the newspaper. How can you read and feel the joy of your food? When I saw a little boy riding a bike and eating a burger, I was sadly surprised. I have seen people eat when they are depressed, sad, mad, angry, unhappy, and nervous. Believe it or not, I have seen people eat when they are completely full. I guess they just eat for the fun of it or as a bad habit, but the result is not much fun.

Eat when you are hungry and stop eating before you get completely full if you want to stay healthy. Make time to eat slowly with joy, and always thank God for his blessings if you want to see more of them.

WOMEN ARE POWERFUL AND INDEPENDENT

I was astonished by women's independence and power in the United States. I realized how some stand up for themselves and their beliefs. How freely they speak their mind, think their own thoughts, and do things their own way. How easily they express what's in their minds and hearts. *They live their lives their ways.*

They won't allow anyone to step on them; and if somebody tries, they stop that person quickly. Whenever there is injustice, they speak against it. They are very outspoken, opinionated, and determined. They go after what they want, and there is nothing that can stop them.

I was happy to see some get the best use of the rights and opportunities available to them in this land of women's rights, and I hope those who don't yet do it will learn to do the same thing.

I noticed that some have the courage and power to allow themselves to be who they truly are and won't become anyone else's idea of what American women should be. They make time for themselves first, instead of others who are more powerful, more independent, and more successful. They have discovered their true value. These are the women who live a better life and are more powerful.

DIVERSITY OF RELIGION

Everybody can stick to their own beliefs and religions; there is religious freedom in America. Sweet! I was pleasantly surprised to witness all kinds of people with different kinds of religions living together in America— Christians, Muslims, Jews, Hindus, Catholics, Buddhists, Zoroastrians, Sufis, and many more.

Some religions were provided by God for our spiritual awareness. Having spiritual beliefs makes us grow stronger and deeper to help heal ourselves and create a better world.

I am an Iranian Muslim. I personally love and respect other religions too, especially the ones that came from God. I think they all talk about being and doing well. I believe religions are important, but more important than that is our personal relationship with God.

When I was about twelve years old and going to middle school, one day one of my friends came over to do our homework together. After a while we reached a question that neither of us knew the answer to. The neighbors' daughter was our classmate too. I recommended we go to her house and ask her. My Muslim friend immediately disagreed. When I asked why, she responded, "They are not Muslim and not clean."

"Why aren't they clean?" I asked.

"Because they are not Muslim," she responded.

"What does cleanliness have to do with not being Muslim? I go there sometimes, and I know they are very clean people," I said.

"I told you, their house may be clean, but they are not clean in heart."

"They are such kind, caring, and good people. How can they be bad in heart? I have never seen anything bad in them," I persisted.

"They are Zoroastrians, and we as Muslims need to stay away from them. We should not eat in their house; we should not be around them," she said.

I became so confused. *What is she talking about?* I asked myself.

Anyway, I decided to go to the neighbors' house and see if my Zoroastrian friend knew the answer. By the time I was back to my house, my Muslim friend was gone.

I talked to my parents about what had happened. My dad said, "There is not such a thing in the Quran. The next time you go to the Zoroastrians' house, pay attention to the symbolic picture on the wall and read the writings on the bottom of the picture."

I had seen the picture before, but I had never paid attention to the writings below it. I rushed back to the neighbors' house and, for the first time, read the writing. It said, *good thoughts, good words,* and *good deeds.* There was nothing wrong about what they believe in. *Why did my Muslim friend think they were bad people?*

Let me tell you a little about Zoroastrianism. The religion, also called Mazdaism, started in the ancient Iranian society of Persia around 648 BC and was spread to China and India via the Silk Road (according to Herodotus's *The Histories,* completed in 440 BC).

According to facts I researched on the Internet, Zoroastrianism was the main religion of Persia until the seventh century, when the Sassanied Dynasty was overthrown by the Arabs and was slowly replaced by Islam. Many believers are still living in the central Iranian states of Yazd and Kerman, and many migrated to Gujarat in western India (today they are called the Paresis).

Being among the oldest religions in human history, Zoroastrianism was copied by other religions, especially the Abrahamian religions of the Middle East and Buddhism in India. Thus it had great influence on human beliefs.

This religion is based on teachings ascribed to Zoroaster, after whom the religion is named. It is based on the worship of Ahura Mazda, the one and only supreme divine authority for its believers. Adherents believe there is a permanent fight between Ahura Mazda (God) and Ahriman (evil), and that at last Ahura Mazda will prevail over Ahriman. That's when time ends, and the Savior will bring about a final renovation of the world. All the dead will be revived. At this time there will be a final purgation of evil from the earth, and each person will be transformed into a spiritual body.

The good thing about Zoroaster was that he concentrated on the good side of the human personality, namely, good thoughts, good words, and good deeds which, if implemented, could lead to happiness for the believers. He chose water and fire as being sacred (agents of virtual purity and life sustaining), and they would be key elements in their prayers.

The holy book of Zoroastrianism is called Avesta in the Avestan language, which is one of the old Iranian languages close to Sanskrit. It consists of seventeen *gathas* (songs for the purpose of prayers), which consist of 238 verses (1,300 lines or 6,000 words total).

I believe a bad person is an evil one, no matter what kind of religion he says he has (actually he has none). We don't need to change our religion to become a better person; we just need to turn our minds and hearts toward God's words and direction to become a better person. I am a Muslim, but I could be a Jew and still be the same person with the same heart. It is not religion that makes people bad; it's people who make the religions look bad.

For instance, the suicide bombers in Afghanistan call themselves Muslims, but in reality they are not Muslims. They are against Islam and hide behind the religion to do their evil acts. They are acting against God's words, which in the Quran dictate peace. If a Christian man by the name BTK from Wichita, Kansas, raped several women after killing them also worked at a church to hide his evil act, would you call him a Christian? Of course not. You would simply call him evil.

I don't blame the religion, and I don't blame the church. I blame the person and his evil act.

Almost all religions have a message of love, sharing, good doing, and peace. If a person hides behind a religion for bad doing, I call that person evil; I don't see his religion as a bad one.

If I see a child-molesting Catholic priest, I don't look at his religion as a bad one. I look at that person as an evil person, with no God or any kind of religion in him. If I see a rapist hiding behind Christianity, I don't think Christianity is a bad religion. I see an evil person with no heart and no God's words in him destroying children's lives. If I see a terrorist hiding behind Islam to do his evil acts, that person definitely is not a Muslim. He is evil, and he acts like one by taking his life and the lives of others. I believe if someone has God and God's words in his mind and heart, he is not capable of doing bad.

I believe even the worst criminals have a beautiful spot in their heart, since they were born clean and innocent as children. That beautiful spot may have been buried with a lot of criminal activities and terrible choices over many years. They just need to rediscover that childhood inner beauty in themselves and bring it out. Criminals are not born; they are made. If a criminal today opens his heart to God and invites God in, he can be forgiven by God according to the Quran; he can return to his childhood innocence.

Religions that came from God are here to make life better, easier, more peaceful, more beautiful, more joyful, and healthier for us; life is easy if we just follow God's laws. Fly higher, go further, dream bigger, and dig deeper in yourself to reach spiritual moments and feel the beauty of it. No matter what kind of religion you have, be a good person and have a good relationship with God. Have a beautiful mind and a great heart and let God shine in your heart.

Seven days without God makes one *weak*.

A good person is a good person; a bad person is an evil one, and it doesn't have anything to do with their religion. Love and respect other religions. Maybe this way a lot of conflicts will wash away from this earth.

A MEETING AGAINST ISLAM

I was invited to a meeting by a friend to talk about my first book (*The Darkest Days of My Life in the U.S. and Iran*), but when I got there, I found out the real purpose of the meeting was to talk against Islam. They started the meeting talking about Muslim extremists and quickly began talking negatively against the Quran. That meeting really surprised me because I had never seen or heard any true believer of Quran insult the other prophets and the other holy books. As a matter of fact, my parents and grandparents always talked good about Jesus. I even remember my mom saying she had Jesus in her heart due to what Allah said in the Quran.

I was the only Muslim among them. Nobody knew but my friend who had asked me to speak about my book. When I was called on to speak, the first thing that came out of my mouth was, "I am a Muslim, and my parents and grandparents were Muslims too. I never saw or heard anything bad about them because they were true Muslims, the kind that God in the Quran asked them to be."

To tell you the truth, I had never read nor paid attention to the Quran before. The only good things I heard and learned about the Quran came from my parents and my other real Muslim friends. That meeting made me wonder; I was shocked. *Are Islam and the Quran as bad as they were saying in that meeting?* I asked myself. I felt a little confused that day to be a Muslim.

But when I thought a little deeper, I realized my parents and grandparents were Muslims and they were wonderful human beings. Something somewhere wasn't making sense. If Islam was as bad as they were saying, why were most of the true believer Muslims I knew good and honest human beings? Studying the Quran was the only way to find the answer to my question.

Today I call that meeting a blessing for me because that meeting opened my eyes. The more I read the Quran, the more I fell in love with Allah and his peaceful words. Today I call myself a true believer of Allah's words in the Quran; today I call myself a true believer of Mohammad, Jesus, Moses, Abraham, Ishmael, Isaac, Jacob, Nuh, Maryam, and all the other prophets whose names are mentioned in the holy book, the Quran. I would have never found out about the true Allah if it hadn't been for that meeting. I would never have found out about my true self if it hadn't been for that meeting. The more I read the Quran, the more it amazed me, especially when I read how the Quran and Muslims respect the other prophets because God said to and because Allah wanted peace on his earth, not conflict.

I absolutely disagree with these kinds of meetings, if there are any anywhere about any religions. How can you insult the Quran when Jesus, Moses, and lots of other prophets are in it? Why is it so hard to tell the truth, but very easy to tell a lie? Why brainwash people in such wicked meetings to believe something that is not true? Nowadays I take more time to remember all that Allah has said and has done for us in the Quran and his other books. Nowadays when I pray, I pray from the bottom of my heart, knowing praying is a free gift, with no cost and wonderful rewards. Nowadays when I pray, I am so awake, but when I watch a movie, I am so sleepy. It used to be the opposite. Nowadays I think more of what Allah thinks of me, not what other people think of me. Again, it used to be just the opposite.

Jesus was all about love, peace, and purity. He likes his true followers to have self-respect but also to respect other religions. He gave up his life and blood to bring love and peace to the earth, as he said, to allow the earth to follow him. If you are the one doing these kinds of meetings, not only are you not following Jesus, but also you are making him uncomfortable. Save this energy, time, and money to spread more love and peace on this earth, as Jesus did, not hatred. Be his true follower and make him proud. Following Jesus is more important than being a Christian.

I absolutely disagree with people who write anti-religious books. I wonder what they want to accomplish. More animosity on God's earth? Are they promoting violence on this earth instead of peace? I have seen anti-Christian books, anti-Islamic books, anti-Judaism books, and many others, but I never read any of them because my time is more valuable than to read something negative and untrue. I would rather read a book that will help me to have a cleaner and more beautiful spirit and to learn something positive in my life. To spread more peace on God's earth. I would rather read and learn more about spreading peace, because God wants us to live in peace and have a good relationship with each other; God does not want any conflict on his earth. Writing anti-religious books is against God's will and his words; it also increases conflict and confusion on his earth. To advertise your religion, you don't need to step on other religions; you just need to be a better person. That will work much better.

I learned how to live a better life from studying the Quran. I was amazed how the Quran mentioned all of God's prophets with love. *Muslims believe in God and that which was revealed unto us, and that which was revealed unto Abraham and Ishmael and Isaac and Jacob and the tribes, and that which was entrusted unto Moses and Jesus and the prophets from their lord; we make no distinction between any of them and unto Him we have submitted* (Quran 3/84).

In the Quran Allah taught me to have self-respect and respect others too. That's why Muslims respect their own religion and also have respect for other religions as well. That's the way it should be if we want peace on this earth. A true Muslim can worship God anywhere—in a mosque, in a Christian church, in a Jewish synagogue … I mean anywhere. God is not only in those places; God is everywhere, and you can worship him any time.

Words of wisdom from the Quran that help in everyone's way of life include:

1. Respect and honor all human beings irrespective of their religion, color, race, sex, language, status, property, birth, and profession/job (17/70).

2. Talk straight, to the point, without any ambiguity or deception (33/70).

3. Choose the best words to speak and say them in the best possible way (17/53, 2/83).

4. Always speak the truth. Shun words that are deceitful or ostentatious (22/30).

5. Do not confound truth with falsehood (2/42).

6. Say with your mouth what is in your heart (3/167).

7. When you voice an opinion, be just, even if it is against a relative (6/152).

8. Do not be a bragging boaster (31/18).

9. Do not talk, listen, or do anything vain (23/3, 28/55).

10. Do not participate in anything paltry. If you pass near a futile play, then pass by with dignity (25/72).

11. Do not verge upon any immodesty or lewdness, whether surreptitious or overt (6/151).

12. *If, unintentionally, any misconduct occurs by you, then correct yourself expeditiously (3/134).*

13. *Do not be contemptuous or arrogant with people. Do not walk haughtily or with conceit (31/18, 17/37).*

14. *Be moderate in thy pace (31/19).*

15. *If you do good, you do it for yourself, and if you do evil, you do it against yourself (17/7).*

16. *If you do not have complete knowledge about someone, keep a favorable view about him/her until you attain full knowledge about the matter. Consider others innocent until they are proven guilty with solid and truthful evidence (24/12–13).*

17. *Ascertain the truth of any news, lest you smite someone in ignorance and afterward repent of what you did (49/6).*

18. *Do not follow blindly any information of which you have no direct knowledge (17/36).*

19. *Never think that you have reached the final stage of knowledge and nobody knows more than yourself. Remember, above everyone endowed with knowledge is another endowed with more knowledge (12/76).*

20. *The true believers are but a single brotherhood. Live like members of one family, brothers and sisters unto one another (49/10).*

21. *Do not make mockery of others or ridicule others (49/11).*

22. *Do not defame others (49/11).*

23. *Do not insult others by nicknames (49/11).*

24. *Avoid suspicion and guesswork. Suspicion and guesswork might deplete your communal energy (49/12).*

25. *Spy not upon one another (49/12).*

26. *Do not backbite one another (49/12).*

27. *When you meet each other, offer good wishes and blessings for safety. One who conveys to you a message of safety and security and also when a courteous greeting is offered to you, meet it with a greeting still more courteous or at least of equal courtesy (4/86).*

28. *Think kindly of your parents, relatives, the orphans, and those who have been left alone in society (4/36).*

29. Take care of the needy, the disabled, those whose hard-earned income is insufficient to meet their need. And those whose businesses have stalled. And those who have lost their jobs (4/36).

30. Think kindly of your related and unrelated neighbors, companions by your side in public gatherings and public transportation (4/36).

31. Be generous to the needy wayfarer, the homeless child of the street, and the one who reaches you in a destitute condition (4/36).

32. Be nice to the people who work under your care. (4/36).

33. Do not follow up what you have given to others to afflict them with reminders of your generosity (2/262).

34. Do not expect a return for your good behavior, not even a thanks (76/9).

35. But those who believe and do righteous Deeds, for them shall be the Permanent Reward of the Paradise (95/6).

36. But for those who forbear and do good, there is Forgiveness and Great Reward (11/11).

37. You should enjoin right conduct on others, but mind your own ways first. Actions speak louder than words. You must first practice good deeds yourself, then preach (2/44).

38. Correct yourself and your families first, before correcting others (66/6).

39. Pardon gracefully if anyone among you commits a bad deed out of ignorance, and then repents and amends (6/54, 3/134).

40. Divert and sublimate your anger and potentially virulent emotions to creative energy, and become a source of tranquility and comfort to people (3/134).

41. Call people to the way of the Lord with wisdom and beautiful exhortation. Reason with them most decently (16/125).

42. Leave to themselves those who do not give any importance to the divine code and have adopted and consider it as mere play and amusement (6/70).

43. Do not be jealous of those who are blessed (4/54).

44. Do not squander your wealth senselessly (17/26).

45. Fulfill your promises and commitments (17/34).

46. Keep yourself clean and pure (9/108, 4/43, 5/6).

47. *Dress up in agreeable attire and adorn yourself with exquisite character from the inside out (7/26).*

48. *Seek your provision only by fair endeavor (29/17, 2/188).*

49. *Allah, through the holy Quran, guides whoever seeks Allah's pleasure to the peace-giving ways, and he takes them out of the darkness toward the light by his will and guides them to the straight path (5/16).*

FROM SURAH 19 MARYAM IN THE QURAN

The Quran mentioned that Mussa was indeed a selected divine emissary and a messenger. Also, God appointed his brother Harun as a messenger to be Mussa's aide. God sent Mussa with signs of miracles to bring people out from darkness.

The Quran mentioned Jesus as the obedient worshipper of God and that God gave him the scripture and has appointed him a messenger.

The Quran mentioned Ismail, son of Ibrahim, that he was true to his promise and he was an emissary and a prophet.

The Quran mentioned Idris as a truthful messenger.

The Quran mentioned Zakariya as God's exclusive worshipper and also Yahya (Zakariya's son) as a divine, knowledgeable prophet from God.

Those mentioned messengers are those whom Allah bestowed His Grace upon. They were offspring of Adam or of those whom were carried in the ship along with Nuh; some of them were the posterity of Ibrahim and Ismail, whom were guided and chosen.

Let me explain a little about Muslim prayers. A Muslim woman wears a head covering as an important part of her spiritual journey. The Muslim prayer, which is over 1400 years old, is repeated five times a day by hundreds of millions of people all around the world. It is not only for spiritual needs but also for connecting with Muslims around the world.

COUNSELING THE CRIMINALS (EVILDOERS)

The most upsetting surprise of all was when some criminals do evil, sometimes instead of jail, they are sent to rehabilitation and counseling. I never understood why.

I am a huge believer of God. I believe God has created each person with a brain in their head to think and use it the best way possible, to know the difference between bad and good, and to make good choices. The most important thing is that God sent his words to tell us how to live a good life. He has no control of our lives—that's the reason he created us with a brain. He also doesn't want anything bad for us, which is why he sent us his laws through his selected prophets to tell us how to live a good and healthy life. If you live God's way, you will find that life will be easier for you. So it is not God who controls our lives or makes bad and good choices for us. It's the brain in our head—it's us.

It is all up to us to make a good choice or an evil one. God has no control of our lives; that's why he gave us a brain to use to find our way. Otherwise he could have created us with no brain and just controlled our lives. It all depends on us. If we do evil, it's our choice, and we need to be punished harshly for it. That's the only way we can stop evildoing.

If someone rapes a little girl, that's his evil choice. He needs to be punished harshly for it. Counseling is a reward for their evil act. If someone became a teacher or nurse of the year, it was their choice. But do they get any reward from lawmakers for it? If someone became the president of the United States, it was his choice of dedication and hard work to be able to help and work for other people. If someone is a very good and honest person, he gets his reward from God. Is there any law in the United States to reward him? Of course not. Why then are there laws in this country to reward some people's evil acts? Aren't our lives made of our choices? Some choose the bad, and they need to pay for it.

I know one thing for sure: if you do good, good comes to you, and if you do bad, all you get is bad—it's as simple as that. If you are a Godly person, life will get easier for you because you will be able to deal with reality better. There is a good and an evil inside each of us; it's all up to us which one to feed. The person who feeds the good becomes a winner. A good person represents a lot; you can see the goodness through his eyes and acts, you can hear the goodness in his voice, and you can feel the goodness in his heart.

There is a difference between an evil person and a crazy one. There are different levels of craziness, but let me tell you of the first time I went to a lunatic asylum and witnessed real crazy people with my own shocked eyes. I used to have a friend who worked at such a place as a nurse. She was at my house visiting one day. All of a sudden she got a phone call from her workplace, and she had to rush back to work for a while. I asked if I could go with her. I have always been curious about different kinds of people and their reactions toward life. I asked how long she was going to stay at the lunatic asylum. She said she would not be long; she just needed to drop off some paperwork at the office. She agreed I could go with her under several conditions: I was not supposed to stare at anybody, I was not supposed to smile at anybody, and I was supposed to have a serious look on my face and walk strongly and quickly.

When we arrived there, the huge and tall double iron door caught my attention. As soon as the door was opened, my heart dropped. For a second I forgot all the recommendations my friend had given me earlier. My friend reminded me very quickly, and I started to follow her to the office. In order to reach the office, we had to pass the yard. My eyes were wide open to what I was witnessing; there was no way I could ignore those people. For some reason, in my eyes they were innocent people chained by their feet and could hardly walk around. I felt for them so badly.

Some were sitting and making weird gestures with their hands. Some were making unusual noises, or maybe it was a way of talking to themselves. None of them were together or even talking with each other. One was nodding his head so badly that I could not help but stare at him. All of them were so involved with their own acts they didn't even notice us. I noticed some crazy people in the hallway chained up when we entered the building. I felt fear inside, maybe because we were closer to them in the building. I had a quick look at each of them, trying not to stare at any of them. I realized one of them smiled at me. I felt bad and smiled right back at him. At that time we were entering the office. I felt safer when we got into the office.

After a little while I saw the guy who I smiled back at was standing outside and staring at me. I panicked and turned my back to him. I looked outside through the window again after a while. He was gone. After a while, he was back at the office door, and trying so hard to come toward me with a big smile on his face, it took three big men to hold him to give him a shot. It did not take long for him to fall asleep. My friend asked me, "What happened?"

"I think only crazy people fall in love with me," I said.

That day was one of the most memorable days of my life because I saw something that I had never witnessed before in my life and probably never will again. I also learned there is a huge difference between crazy people and evil people. Since then I never call an evil person a crazy one because I don't like to insult the crazy people. A crazy person isn't able to look after himself, but an evil person can. Crazy people do things without thinking and unintentionally, yet evil people go by a plan and they are completely aware of what they are doing. An evil person can make a choice, but choices don't exist for the crazy ones. I realized the crazy people have no control of their brains, yet evil ones do. There is a huge difference between an evil person who can think and make choices and a crazy person who can't.

If we feed our children's minds with beautiful thoughts at an early age, their attitudes become beautiful too. If we treat our children with respect, love, attention, and care, they won't turn evil later in life. Raise your children responsibly. Focus on God, rather than material things, and he will come through for you and your family. All things are possible to the believer.

MARRIAGE COUNSELING

Another thing that really surprised me: first people get married, some cheat on each other, some abuse each other verbally and physically, some then separate for a time. At the end, they have no more energy to fight. They decide to go to counseling and solve their problems.

Isn't it easier and healthier to get counseling first, then start a healthy relationship?

OBESITY

Oh boy, I could write an entire book about this surprising problem in America. I had very beautiful thoughts about thin and beautifully formed American people before I came to the United States. My thoughts were centered around women mostly. I honestly thought all American women looked like Barbie. I thought it would be boring if all American women did look like Barbie. When I arrived to America and witnessed the first several overweight people, I thought they were not Americans. I could not speak or understand English at the beginning, but I was always a good observer.

When I started to pay attention to people's grocery shopping carts, I realized almost all of them were loaded with chips, dips, candies, cookies, all different kinds of sugared colas, a lot of ribs, pork, red meat, and lots more unhealthy food. I noticed black people's shopping carts were loaded with more unhealthy food compared to those of white people. That's how I found out the reason for obesity in this country—by checking out grocery shopping carts. Those who are overweight and obese—67 percent of the population, according to news reports—pay for quantity of food, not quality.

It really shocked me that Americans were more willing to spend money on health issues that resulted from eating unhealthy food than to spend it buying quality food. Most people don't work out, they aren't active, they eat unhealthy foods, they don't care what they put in their mouths, they eat just to fill up their stomachs, they eat a lot, and they don't have enough knowledge about healthy foods.

It also surprised me when the first day I went to the YMCA to exercise; I saw children and teenagers with candy bars and sodas in their hands. Even at an exercise place, they sell candy bars and colas! I went to the room that had all those vending machines and looked in the machines. Mostly they were selling unhealthy foods and drinks rather than healthy ones.

In my opinion, there shouldn't be any—I mean none—especially at a place that represents health, happiness, and staying fit. It doesn't make sense. We encourage our kids to exercise, but at the same time to not eat healthy. They get confused. People can't forget about candy bars and colas even at an exercise place. I would be much happier if I couldn't find any salt, sugar, and unhealthy fats there.

Vendors use fattening sauces in their food or on their sandwiches to make the food taste better and sell quicker; instead, they should use delicious herbs, spices, and olive oil. In sixteen years of living in the United States, I have never ever seen a bag of turmeric or cumin or fennel or a lot of other spices and herbs in any American's shopping cart. Such spices and herbs are real brain foods and very healthy to eat.

Research on the Internet shows that obesity costs Americans a trillion dollars a year. Sixty-seven percent of Americans are fat, and this number is growing just like the size of the waist of fat men and women in this country. Sometimes when I give my children advice, they are good listeners but not doers. If an outsider tells them the same thing that I have already told them, they listen and do it as well. So I have realized that an outsider's advice often has a better effect than an insider's. It doesn't matter how many times insiders like the media talk about fat people in America or write books about them—the people don't get it, or it just has no effect on them. Maybe they'll believe an outsider like me and do something about the extra fat that they are carrying around.

The sad thing about fat children in America is the food parents buy and prepare at home, the food children are being fed at schools, the food restaurants—especially fast-food ones—sell, and what the food companies make for people—all of these sources provide unhealthy food. Children have no choice but to eat whatever you as parents and the school give them.

The most surprising thing was the parents. Whatever we buy and make, then put in front of the children, whatever snack we put on the coffee table, they grab and eat it. Whatever wrong choices we make, not only do our children pay for it, but also we and the country pay for it. Nine times out of ten, obesity depends on *your* choices of buying and eating, the choices you make for yourself and your family. Obesity is a serious life-threatening disease. You would be amazed what you can accomplish just by buying right and eating right. Eating right has a direct connection with thinking right. Can you realize what a huge impact you as parents can have on decreasing obesity simply by buying healthy?

When a mother of an eight-hundred-pound son (on Oprah's show, March 26, 2009) said it is hard to say no to children when they want something to eat, I was freaked out. The first step is to learn to say no to ourselves; then it would be easier to say no to the kids. When we go grocery shopping, we need to say no to all the unhealthy food. Then we need to have a nutrition food schedule on the kitchen wall and follow up. We should also get the children involved and ask their opinion. Kids like to help; it makes them feel like they are important.

Nobody said you should starve your children; all I am asking is that you feed their bodies and minds with nutritious food. It will make you as a parent happier. You won't have to watch your eight-hundred-pound son suffer and not be able to go out, go to school, play with his friends, take a shower, move about, sit on a chair like a normal kid, and enjoy his one life that he deserves to enjoy. Every breath he takes, he thinks it's his last one. All he does is lie on the bed and wait for death to come to him. Isn't this worth saying no to yourself and your demanding son? Of course. What will make you satisfied and happy as a parent? What about watching your son have a normal weight and normal life and do whatever a happy kid does?

The good thing is for you to admit to your mistake. After you do that, I can hope and pray for a change. Children look up to their parents for a lot of things. Don't be an irresponsible parent. If you are, you are just going to hurt your family and yourself. Don't buy nasty, unhealthy, good-looking groceries that are like poison for your mind and body. The more you buy these unhealthy groceries, the more companies are going to make them. They don't care about you, your family, the diseases, and the obesity; all they care about is getting your money and making a profit. We as buyers have direct control of the food producer by buying their product; don't forget that we vote for the product we buy. If we quit buying their unhealthy product, they will quit making it. Let's do it.

Always avoid two words: *can't* and *impossible*. We *can* do it together for ourselves, our family, our country, and our world. It is possible, and we can do it. Let me mention that obesity doubled in the past two decades, obesity increased 37 percent from 1996 to 2008, and childhood obesity has tripled since 1980 (these facts are all easily found on the Internet). This is an alarming situation. Twenty-five million obese children live in America; this is a crime that parents and schools are responsible for. Who buys the food? Who prepares the food? Who feeds the children? We as parents do. The children are the victims of our lack of education and information about healthy eating habits. FOX News has reported that Americans eat twenty-two teaspoons of sugar every day, mostly in colas, and type 2 diabetes is growing among innocent obese children. This is a crime, don't you agree?

Let me tell you something interesting that I experienced long ago. One day I, my family, and several friends got together to watch a movie. I put some donuts, chips, cookies, dried fruit, and colas on the coffee table. Everybody grabbed something to eat as soon as they got situated. By the end of the movie, there was nothing left. I could not resist the temptation myself, so I also had some donuts and cola because that's what was in front of me.

It took awhile before we got together again. This time I prepared a dish of vegetables, including cherry tomatoes, celery, cauliflower, and carrots. I added some olive oil and lime juice to a healthy fat-free dip. I also served a dish of fruit with cantaloupe, pineapple, grapes, and strawberries, as well as some oatmeal walnut sugar-free cookies. I placed everything on the coffee table as soon as the movie started. Everybody first reached for the fruit and cookies, and then they started to work on the vegetable dish. Again, by the end of the movie there was nothing left on the coffee table. When I noticed all the healthy food was gone, I felt a kind of joy inside. This is a habit we give our kids, and they grow with it. Let them grow with the good habits that we give them.

It's all up to us as parents what we buy, what we cook, what we store in the refrigerator, what we hide in the pantry, and what we place on the dining and coffee tables. We raise fat kids and then label them as fat, lazy, stupid, and dumb. When you label your kid with bad names, they truly believe in their heart and mind they are entitled to it. Never give your children wrong labels, because it encourages them to wrongdoing, just as positive labels encourage them to success.

We as parents have an enormous duty toward our children and their lives. What we do matters. Every crisis and problem has a turning point, and it's possible you just need to make a good choice. Believe me, if you feed yourself and your family in a healthy way, a lot of your problems are going to disappear. You will become happy, healthy, energetic, smart, and spiritual.

Remember: being part of something special makes you feel special, so become a special parent for your special children.

SPIRITUALITY AND OUR CHILDREN

Spirituality is a unique relationship and connection between our soul and God. It's heavenly beyond the material world and bodily senses. It involves an intimate relationship with God, talking to him as one's best friend. Spirituality plays a central role in self-help and developing inner peace, abilities, and activities. I believe there is a connection between spirituality and being religious.

Spirituality doesn't know place or time. Some people become spiritual when they go to their praying places, like churches, mosques, or other holy places. Others get spiritual when listening to music, playing a musical instrument, singing, or writing. Some get spiritual when they look at the sky and nature, and some when they are alone or in the darkness or listen to religious music. Others get spiritual when they are in love or in pain. Some get spiritual when they have many problems in their life or need a beyond-human help, something to hold on to, to help them get rid of the grief.

We need to feed our children's spiritual needs for their own good. The closer they get to knowing God, the better they can handle their problems later in life.

Our children have become so involved with computers, games, TV, and cell phones; they don't even see and feel the beauty of nature. They don't hear singing birds or the showering noise of a rain on a river or the beautiful crystal drops of rain. They don't even see and sense the smell of different colorful beautiful flowers. Do they even know there is a sky above their heads? I look at the sky a lot. It relaxes me spiritually. It also keeps me busy, especially when there are clouds in the sky. I use my imagination to make different shapes out of the clouds. Sometimes cloud shapes are like mushrooms, boats, buffalo, human faces, trees, simple houses, fish, and lots of other things. Blue and white—what a relaxing and beautiful color combination!

I am usually asleep for the sunrise, but my eyes are always wide open when the sun goes down. Sunset is never the same, especially when there are clouds in the sky. God, I love you and thank you for all the colorful beauty in nature that you have created for us. I am very sure there are kids that haven't seen the stars in the sky at night. It is so beautiful, it takes your breath away when you look at all that beauty, the beauty that most of our children don't even know exists. Because they don't have time for nature.

When I was a child, we slept outside in the summer. I couldn't wait to go to bed and look at the sky, stars, and moon. Bedtime was the happiest time of my day. I had named some of the stars and talked to them, told them about my day and stories until I went to sleep. Sometimes I woke up in the middle of the night and was scared because everybody else was asleep. Then I asked the biggest star to watch me until I went back to sleep again, so I wasn't scared anymore and went to sleep in peace. I still do that—go out and look at the sky, stars, and moon. They remind me of God's power.

The Internet, video games, and cell phones have stolen our children's time and happiness; they are missing the reality of life. All these things have limited their thoughts and time (mind-sets); they look tired and feel depressed. They need to be reminded that nature makes them happy, relaxed, healthy, energetic, spiritual, and beautiful minded. They don't pay attention to their bodies and souls as much as they do to their "toys"—television, video games, cell phones, and the Internet. They have no spiritual connection, and they have forgotten about themselves. We need to remind them their lives get improved by being spiritual and connecting to God. They will find a peaceful mind by having a relationship with God. They also discover themselves better as they fall deeper into their spiritual mode.

We can't find true satisfaction and happiness in life unless we find our true creator. We can't achieve happiness without obeying God's words. If you have tried all the other things to get rid of the pain in your mind and heart, give God a chance. Try him, and you will feel his presence and peace in you; he is above kindness and always welcomes you.

You are who you decide you want to be. A beautiful house, a nice car, and a boat don't give you true happiness; your pure relationship with your creator does. Try it! Most people don't realize the real meaning of freedom is to be free of the material world, to be free of negative thoughts. The real meaning of freedom is being free of the evil inside us, being free of drugs and alcohol. To achieve real freedom, we need to work on having a great relationship with our creator, having beautiful thoughts and a free spirit.

Not all angels have wings. I have seen and met real angels living on this earth with no wings. God has blessed us with lots of things in nature and in us. He has blessed us with a pair of eyes to look at beautiful things, a pair of ears to listen to beautiful things, two legs to go to beautiful places, two hands to do beautiful things for ourselves and others, a heart to feel beautiful things as well as the real pain of needy people, a brain to think and choose God's way and put beautiful things in it, and a tongue to say beautiful things. There are angels living on this earth who do all these things.

I look at a negative person as a damaged brain. A negative person's brain is like a cluttered room: the more trash you dump and keep in that room, the more depressing it gets. When you start to get rid of the clutter and the trash, you open more space for beautiful things. The more garbage you take out, the more space you open for new and beautiful things.

If you replace the garbage with colorful beautiful flowers and paint the room with a light attractive color and hang some peaceful real pictures of nature, the room becomes more relaxing and peaceful and it brings you joy. You need to do the same thing with your negative thoughts; get rid of them and replace them with positive and beautiful thoughts. What we believe matters. If we believe in God's words, things change.

What do you get from negativity? Depression, hate, hopelessness, anger, loneliness, anxiety, low self-esteem, and a damaged brain.

What do you get from positivity? Peace comes over you; a peaceful mind makes you happy. Being peaceful and spiritual brings out the best and unknown in you. It will create closeness and unity with God. Our family and friends also help us to progress toward what we need to achieve in life. Life cares about what you need, not what you want. You enjoy a peaceful and beautiful mind just as you enjoy having a beautiful and peaceful room.

You help heal and create a better world when you are spiritual. Forgiveness is the first step toward spirituality; forgiveness keeps you away from anger, hatred, and waste of spirit. Forgive and forget your past; forgive your friends, your family, and your enemy for your own sake and move on with peace. Warm and giving hands, a kind heart, and a beautiful mind help you to lift your spirit. Live for today. Sometimes today comes with problems, issues, sorrow, deception, and tears; other times it comes full of surprises, happiness, success, and achievements. It's not always what we ask for, but it's present to teach us how to learn, grow, and do the best for ourselves and others. We need to welcome the bad as well as the good in our lives; you never know, maybe bad will do us more good than bad at the end. Every day appreciate God's giving with enthusiasm and love. Train your brain to stay positive. Practicing yoga trains your brain to stay focused on your body's movement and breathing. It also promotes relaxation and brings the stress level down in you and your body.

Stress comes from negativity and destroys the brain's abilities. If you want to keep your brain sharp, try to create ways to get rid of stress in you. Meditation is another powerful key to having a powerful, positive, and peaceful mind. Both yoga and meditation require concentration and focus. They also keep the oxygen level rich in your blood, which helps you to have a healthy, sharp, focused, and spiritual brain. Sometimes we don't know why we do things we do—that's one of the times we need to ask for God's help.

Natural, God-made food also makes you spiritual, energetic, happy, sharp, positive, and closer to God. We call such foods brain food. Unhealthy foods make you fat, depressed, sad, and lazy and keep you away from God.

My grandma had learned from her mom to start the day with being thankful to God, and then take a spoonful of olive oil and a glass of water with several drops of lemon juice. My mom followed her grandma's footsteps. We always had the most complete meal of the day for breakfast. Tea was always mixed with cardamom, ginger, cinnamon, pepper, or any other kind of spice powder. Breakfast included boiled eggs, honey, milk, walnuts, grapes, dates, goat cheese, and goat butter. We always had all kinds of nuts on the breakfast table.

I remember even when we were going to school, my mom would put some walnuts, pistachios, and almonds mixed with raisins in a little plastic bag and place it in our school bag. Other times she gave us homemade dried fruit mixed with all kinds of nuts. She usually gave us oranges, apples, and bananas as fresh fruit to take to school. She always insisted we eat an apple a day, and my problem was I didn't like apples. But knowing it was good for me, I tried to eat it most of the time.

The other habit in our family was eating all kinds of herbs and spices with food. There was always a full dish of mint, parsley, basil, radishes, green onions, and other herbs that would go with lunch and dinner.

We had to have yogurt on the lunch and dinner table every single day. I never saw my grandma or my mom make food without adding turmeric, onion, and garlic to it. They always encouraged us to eat healthy, eating lots of fruit and all kinds of beans and vegetables, especially spinach. They believed eating spinach, lentils, and fish can reverse memory loss. They used to tell us to eat less; they believed eating less would make us be smarter, think better, and have more energy. I remember for years and years my parents ended the night with a hot cup of chamomile with honey.

Eat food high in antioxidants; they protect your body and brain cells. Some of the foods high in antioxidants are dark purplish–colored fruit like prunes, raisins, and all kinds of berries, as well as garlic, kale, and all dark green–colored vegetables.

Eating fish helps to improve concentration. Olive oil, vitamins E and C, nonfat yogurt, avocados, bananas, and cantaloupes are also brain food. Brown rice, chicken, peas, tuna, oatmeal, turkey, and almost all kinds of herbs and spices—like rosemary, oregano, ginger, pepper, basil, marjoram, sage, fennel, bay leaves, parsley, thyme, garlic, onion, cinnamon, cumin, turmeric, cardamom, and a lot more—are also brain food. Herbs and spices have antiaging, anti-inflammatory, and antioxidant effects. In my country, Iran, herbs and spices are prized throughout the country, mostly as medicinal drugs and for health purposes.

There is evidence that the following foods are bad for your brain and give you brain fog: artificial coloring in food, artificial sweeteners, colas, corn syrup, frostings, high sugar drinks, hydrogenated fats, sugars, white bread, and all white flour products. I insist on avoiding sugar (which also gives you wrinkles). Any simple carbohydrate can give you brain fog. Avoid pastas, potato chips, saturated fat, and trans fats. Reduce the amount of salt you take with your food; instead, you can add lime or lemon juice or some apple cider vinegar. Sugar, salt, and bad fats like saturated fat are the worst things you can put into your body.

Constipation causes brain fog; it's not just what goes in but what comes out that is important to brain function. Fiber in legumes, beans, and walnuts is the key to avoiding this problem.

There are other things you can do to improve your brain, such as breathing deeply. Any exercise that affects physical health in a positive way will help the brain too. Good sleep is also important; the quality of sleep is more important than the quantity. A good sleep makes your brain function better. Read, use your dead time to solve puzzles, walk, and spend more time in nature. Be creative, because creativity gives power to your thinking to learn and create new things. Avoid any arguments, especially with people who have their own rules; this save your precious time and energy. The best way to win an argument is to avoid it. Hang out with intelligent and creative people and have them as role models in your mind, asking questions, praying, laughing, playing, dancing, and singing. Do things you enjoy and that make you happy; have a free spirit. Staying positive and being spiritual or religious can help stimulate your brain.

Writing is good for your mind in many ways. It's a way to remind your memory what is important; in this way, you can recall things more easily in the future. It's also a way to clarify your thinking and a way to exercise your creativity and abilities. Diaries, journals, poetry, note-taking, and story-writing are all ways to use writing to improve your brainpower. Besides that, the writer has to do lots of research about the writing subject. If you are interested in writing, make sure to write about what you are not but want to be. For instance, if you are not spiritual but you want to be, write about it; or if you are fat and would like to be thin and healthy, write about how to become thin and healthy. When you start to write about how to be thin and healthy, you need to do a lot of research to educate yourself. When you have the knowledge about how to lose weight and stay healthy, you will probably lose weight by the time you are done with your book.

If you don't know how to cook, start writing a book about it; after all the research, you will become a good cook at the end. If you are suffering from low self-esteem, write about it; write a book about how to be strong and challenge life's problems, how to achieve self-confidence, and how to believe in yourself and the hidden abilities in you. Believe me, by the end of the book, you will be surprised how much confidence you have.

If you are a drug addict, write about how to get clean and free. If you are an angry person, the only way you can find out what anger does to you and how to get over it is to research and write about it; at the end of your writing, you won't feel any anger in you because you have the knowledge of what it does to you. If you are sad and depressed, write about how to challenge depression and become happy. If you are suffering from lack of sleep, do research and write about it. You don't need therapy to solve your problems; you just need to write a book about what you want to be in life. Writing is the best therapy to overcome your problems and negativity.

A problem stays with us in life because of lack of knowledge, but when we educate ourselves, we don't have the problem anymore. Knowledge is power. When we know better, we do better. As I said, write about whatever you are not but want to be. Writing gives you knowledge and power. When you educate yourself, you feel better about you, and it also gives your brain exercise and keeps it sharp. Writing opens up your mind about the reality and truth of life. Writing is like meditating, and it gives you a joyful feeling. When I write, I feel like I am traveling to a spiritual zone that I don't want to come out of. Reading good books can have the same result. When you own a brain that functions better, you draw closer to God and become more spiritual.

DRIVE-THROUGH PICKUPS

The drive-through windows at fast-food restaurants, banks, and drugstores really amazed me. I didn't think that many people would come to drive-through windows for their food when I started to work at McDonald's, but I was wrong. People just don't like to get out of their cars in the heat, cold, wind, rain, snow, and storms—or when they are rushed, tired, sick, lazy, or have their dogs in the car. These are reasons that make drive-through businesses more successful than inside ones.

I sure was glad not to see drive-throughs at grocery stores. At least people have to walk around and get a little exercise when they shop for their groceries.

HAVING RELATIONSHIPS OUTSIDE OF MARRIAGE

There are lots of men and women having relationships outside of their marriages in America. When I watched Oprah in the middle of 2008, what I saw and heard shocked me.

A couple holding hands and looking happy had two children, who also appeared on the show. The married woman had a relationship outside of her marriage, and her husband had no problem with that. The shocking thing was the woman's boyfriend would come to her house during the time the husband and children were home, then they would go to the bedroom and do their thing. How sad!

If we don't know what we want, why get married and make a shaky family foundation? If we got married and found out that's not what we wanted, there are always right ways to solve the problems without confusing and hurting the children. Sometimes separating and divorcing is less hurtful and harmful for the children. Seek counseling. If it doesn't work, get a divorce.

Don't you think getting a divorce is less harmful than sleeping with another man in their dad's bed in your children's presence? The value of a family should be much higher and stronger than that. Oprah was shocked too. At the end she asked the lady, "Aren't you happy you live in America?"

It's people's choices that make this free country stronger or weaker. Some people make the best choices and the best use of living in a free world to make this free land a better place for themselves, their family, and the future of this country. Yet some use freedom to hurt and harm themselves, their family, and this great land of freedom.

SOME AMERICANS DON'T RESPECT THEIR PRESIDENT

The world's most powerful man, Obama. Making fun of the president of the most powerful country in a fun way is fun and beautiful, but disrespecting him is disrespecting your flag, your country, and yourself, unless you don't belong to this country. The people who disrespect their president are against their country, America. Opposing your president is okay in a free country, but name-calling in front of the world is damaging America's reputation.

Strongly disagreeing with your president or not liking him is all good in a free country, but disrespecting him—no matter how much you dislike him—is only going to damage yourself and destroy your country in the eyes of real Americans and the world. Freedom of speech is good as long as it helps America, not hurts it. Some Americans use freedom of speech against America. Shouting and yelling at your president is bad enough; calling him a liar in the eyes of the world is just out of line. What do you think real Americans and the whole world think of you?

WORKING AT A FAST-FOOD RESTAURANT

I am so joyful and proud of myself for making honest and honorable money to feed myself and raise three boys in a free country. I have worked at McDonald's for thirteen years, and I loved every single day of it. I personally love and respect all honorable jobs because our society needs all kinds of people doing different jobs. I believe it is not your job that brings you respect and trust, but your integrity, honesty, and good manner. Money doesn't buy respect for you; your honesty does, by following God's words. We witness so many cases where the CEOs of the biggest companies end up in jail due to stealing and cheating innocent people. Love and respect people for who they are, not what they do. My parents taught me that ever since I was a little girl. I witnessed my parents respect the trash man in the neighborhood the same way they treated and respected the family doctor. As I got older, I realized not very many people do that.

One day as I walked to school with several of my friends, my mom walked with us part of the way. In those days trash men pushed a four-wheel big box by hand, and people put their bags of trash out early every morning for them to dump in that four-wheel box and take away. Sometimes people did not put their trash out early enough, and the trash man would call so loudly for them to bring out the trash that he woke everybody up. We saw a trash man on the way to school, so my mom greeted him nicely. When we got to school, two of my friends made fun of me, saying a trash man is nobody and smells bad and that we should not say hi to him.

As a little girl, I became confused. When I got home, I asked my mom, "Why did you embarrass me by saying hi to the trash man in front of my friends?"

After my mom found out about what happened at school that day, she said she would talk to my friends. The next day she joined us on our way to school.

She asked us to sit on the grass for a minute so she could have a little chat with us. We all sat on the grass and waited to hear what she was going to say.

She began with, "My beautiful little girls, every single job is respectable and honorable as long as people do it in an honest and right way. When we are sick, we see a doctor; he helps our sickness go away. The trash man's job is just as important as a doctor's. The trash man makes the environment clean in order for us not to get sick. They both play a huge role in making our community and us healthy and happy."

As soon as she was done talking and we got ready to walk toward school, we saw the trash man taking the trash away from the neighborhood. This time everybody raced to say hi to him, and I noticed the smile of an angel on my mom's face. Since then I realize how important every single person and their job is.

I started to pay more attention to the people who work really hard but don't get our love and attention just because of our lack of knowledge and our selfishness. Try to replace the selfishness with selflessness; it will make you feel much better about yourself and others. Remember, it doesn't matter how fast you are going as long as you are moving in an honorable and God's direction. Make sure to have a respectful relationship with all kinds of people with different jobs and teach your children too for a more beautiful and easier life in the future. A selfish person with a rude attitude has no place in the community. Good attitude is everything; God will love you, so will the people around you, and you will also like yourself much better. Don't forget that every single honorable job plays a huge role in moving our community ahead.

As I said, I worked at McDonald's for years. I have seen and heard it all. Some of my friends were embarrassed to hang out with me because of my job.

For years I worked two jobs from seven in the morning to twelve or one in the morning nonstop. I never asked for taxpayers' money; I never asked for money from my wealthy parents or anybody else. Every single penny I made proved to myself that I was able and could do something on my own in an honest way. When I ate, I felt the real taste of the food. When I bought something for my children, I felt a real joy in my heart. Every single penny I spent, I felt very good about it. I call it honest or halal money, which was gained in difficult and hard work but the right way—that's all that matters.

I don't care what selfish people think of me because I worked hard at a fast-food restaurant. I care more how I fed my family with honest money and how I feel about myself and the joy inside me. I don't need to prove to any selfish person anything as long as I keep walking in God's direction. I have been ignored by some ignorant people just because of my job. What about me? Why do some of us choose material things and money over life's realities? These things bothered me because I felt bad for some people who are so unaware of the real purpose of life. They raise their innocent children the same way. A real friend is an angel with no wings; a real friend loves you for who you are, not what you do or how much money you have.

There was one incident that happened at McDonald's that captured my attention for some time. It was a typical day at McDonald's. Suddenly I heard a nice, soft voice of a little boy telling one of my employees, "My dad said all the people who work at McDonald's are stupid."

I could not believe what I had heard, but by the way the employee looked at me, I believed my ears. I was worried about my employee's reaction, but after I whispered to him, "I will take care of it; he is just a kid," he was calmer. At first I was going to ignore the whole thing, but I changed my mind quickly, knowing there was a little boy involved. I remember my mom's saying, "If you can save a little boy's mind, you can save his future. It doesn't matter whose kid it is."

I realized there were four boys from maybe age eight to twelve and a middle-aged gentleman together. My employee, Andrew, who was still shocked, approached me and asked, "What are you going to do?

"I will find a way to talk to the little boy," I said. Thankfully Andrew was very understanding and realized that little boy wasn't guilty.

I had to be so careful about how to talk to that little boy. I honestly couldn't let it go without doing anything, knowing that little boy would grow up with those negative thoughts. He was the one who would get hurt and blamed for what his dad had taught him. I was determined to replace his disturbing thoughts with positive ones.

They went to the play area to eat, and I stood behind the counter waiting for them to finish eating. After a while I went to the play area and pretended to clean the tables. The way they were talking, I realized that gentleman wasn't the little boy's dad. That made my job easier and less stressful. After they were done eating, I decided to wait until they were done playing too. I didn't want to interrupt their playful moments. During this time I went to the play area three times, pretending each time that I was cleaning. I also smiled at the little boy. I noticed he was a very happy and sharp boy.

Finally they were done playing. I went back to the play area. The little boy was putting his shoes on. I was a little nervous. I did not want to hurt his feelings or make him think I was against him; I wanted him to feel I was for him and cared about him. The gentleman with them was talking to one of the other boys when I approached the little boy with a smile and asked him if he had fun.

"Of course I did," he said.

I asked if he liked McDonald's.

"It's my favorite place," he answered.

I could see his sharpness in his eyes. "You are a very smart nice young man, and I would love to see you here at McDonald's more often," I said.

All of a sudden, he said, "I love McDonald's. I would like to work here when I'm older. But my dad thinks people who work at McDonald's are stupid."

By then the gentleman and the other boys were listening to our conversation.

The boy said, "My dad is a jerk for saying something like that."

"No, he is not a jerk, he just doesn't know," I replied quickly.

That little boy was so smart, pure, honest, and innocent (aren't all the children?) that I could talk and listen to him for hours without realizing the time passed. Anyway, I taught him what I was taught by my mom as a little girl, about respecting people for who they are, not what they do for a living. The whole time he stood there and listened.

Finally he said, "I love the food, the fries, and the play area at McDonald's. My dad is wrong about people who work at McDonald's. People who work at McDonald's are smart and nice."

Believe me, I could hear such a compliment from an adult and not get excited, but hearing it from an innocent and smart boy made me believe it. He also said that as soon as he turned to working age, he was going to start working at McDonald's.

I gave him a hug and reminded him how smart and beautiful he was. That little boy brought tears of joy to my eyes. The gentleman that was with them apologized to me and Andrew, and they left. I wasn't seeking an apology; I just wanted to get rid of harmful thoughts in his little head.

We as parents kill our children's beautiful thoughts and replace them with our own sick, negative, dangerous, and harmful thoughts. How sad! Today's children are tomorrow's wives, husbands, mothers, and fathers. Raise them well.

My mom used to say, "Learn the knowledge of others and teach yours to others." Make time for what's really important in your life—children. Keep in mind that kids are kids. All children are as sweet and innocent as yours; have care and love for all of them.

Let me tell you about another incident at McDonald's. The lobby door opened, and four boys ages about seven to eleven rushed inside. I noticed one of the boys was very bossy and commanding, and another one was very quiet, innocent looking, and kind of shy. Three of them were talking and having fun, ignoring the quiet one.

The head of the group (the commander) started to order food for himself and the others. Mostly he was making choices for them; if they asked for something, he would disagree and make sure they went by his decisions. The quiet one was standing a little away from them but watching every move they were making. The phone rang, and I had to go to the back room to answer it.

They were eating in the lobby by the time I came back. Two of them and the commander were sitting at a booth, and the quiet one was sitting on a chair but close to them. At first I thought he wasn't eating because he was not hungry. Then I saw the commander pick up a fry and hold it to the quiet boy's face, saying, "These fries are really good." Then he put it in his own mouth. I realized the quiet little boy might be hungry.

The other three, especially the commander, were bullying the quiet one right in front of my eyes—a big mistake. I could feel the blood running to my face, and my ears were getting warm. I was mad. The quiet one had a sad look on his face, which made me more concerned. The others were very loud, and this gave me an excuse to open a conversation with them. I approached and asked them not to be so loud. The commander gave me a funny smile but said nothing. I went back behind the counter.

The commander whispered to the other two, and very soon they were loud again. This time I approached them and asked the quiet one why he wasn't eating.

"I didn't have any money," he said.

"Are you hungry?" I asked.

"Very much," he replied.

I returned to the counter and asked my employee for a cheeseburger, a small fries, and a small drink, which I then took to the boy. He was so surprised and mentioned again that he had no money.

I said, "Don't worry; it's on McDonald's." I witnessed the brightest smile on a little boy's face ever. It just melted my heart.

I left them by themselves to see what the commander was going to do. All three of them that were done with their food approached the quiet one and sat very close to him. He invited the other three to share his fries. I was shocked, and his generosity brought tears to my eyes.

I found a good opportunity to say something to that polite little boy while he was surrounded by the other three. I told him, "You are the most polite, nicest, and best-behaved young man I have ever seen. That food was your reward."

One thing I couldn't understand was why such a wonderful little boy was hanging out with the others, who were nothing compared to him. Thankfully everything became smoother. They spent ten more minutes in the restaurant, talking, laughing, and having fun, all four of them together. They were the center of our attention, and I was following every move they were making. I could not believe how quickly the other three became nice. All children are innocent and nice; they just need some encouragement and somebody to show them the right way.

When they were leaving the restaurant, I gave each of them a little ice cream and told them it was their reward for being nice. Several minutes later, we watched them playing together by the side of the parking lot. How easy it is to talk to children. Sometimes we as parents make it hard for them. Remember: we don't always have to tell them; we can show them too. Words matter, but sometimes our actions speak louder than our words.

Let me share one more incident from work. It was a slow day, and everybody was standing around and talking to each other. Among the employees there was a seventeen-year-old black girl that I admired very much. The reason she had my admiration was that despite being pregnant, she worked hard, was very wise about spending her money, was going to school, and was going to training classes to learn how to give birth to the baby and how to take care of the baby after birth. She was very polite, extremely smart, energetic, very dedicated, and always wore a beautiful smile. She worked hard to get her driver's license and bought her own car. The day after she gave birth to the baby, she attended her graduation party.

Anyway, we were standing around and talking. I heard she was hoping for her baby to have light-colored skin. It surprised me a little, so I turned to her and said, "You need to hope and pray for a healthy and smart baby first. Also, stick to your values and accept and be happy with who you are. Otherwise you won't be happy for the rest of your life." I told her, "I am an Iranian Muslim, and I am proud of it."

She looked at me and said, "But I don't like dark-skinned babies."

I quickly responded, "It is not in your hands and it's not your choice, so let's just pray you have a healthy baby. That's all that matters. Be proud of who you are and where you come from."

I later joked with her and said, "You can't change the color of your skin unless you have millions of dollars like Michael Jackson."

Later, after she had her baby, she told me she was proud of her baby no matter what color the baby was.

In yet another incident from work, one of my employees was so excited to learn my language, Farsi. I told him that in order for him to learn better and memorize the words, I would teach him one word a day. I taught him *Salam* on the first day, meaning hi. On the second day, I taught him *chtori?*

which means "How are you?" I also made sure he remembered the first word that I had taught him the day before. On the third day, as soon as I came in, he said, "Salam, chtori?" I was impressed.

We started talking about cooking all kinds of meat. When I told him about goat and lamb meat, he asked me what lamb was in Farsi. I said *barreh*. He kept repeating the word to memorize it. On the fourth day, when I came in, he told me, "Salam, chtori barreh?" I and Amin, another Iranian working there, laughed for a long time about that employee's cute accent and talking in Farsi.

A ninety-year-old man, very sharp and aware, walked in. I could see life in his eyes; he was very engaging and funny. I asked if he was driving.

"No, I walked," he said.

"It's raining and is also a little cloudy," I said.

"It doesn't bother me; I love rain," he responded.

"You must live close by," I said.

"I live a block away," he told me.

I said, "You are very sharp for your age."

He said, "A nineteen-year-old man should be sharp and aware."

We both started to laugh. He ordered two hamburgers and left the store. I went toward the window to see how fast he was walking in the rain. I noticed that he walked to a tree and sat on the ground next to a dog, gave one hamburger to the dog, and started eating the other one himself. I wished I had a camera to take their picture. I stood by the window and watched them the whole time they were eating.

I went outside after they were done eating and asked him questions about the dog. It seemed he was living with that dog, and the way he was talking about the dog showed his love for the animal. I played with his dog a little, and we said good-bye to each other. As he left, he turned back and said, "And besides my dog, I love women too."

I have so many sweet memories of working at McDonald's that I could write an entire book about it. I told you, I have the best job. No matter what you do, you can always make the best of it.

POLITICS

I was sadly surprised by the dishonesty of some politicians toward their wives and family. When I found out some of them live a secret life and cheat on their wives, yet at the time of confession their wives stand next to them to show support of their husband's act, I was shocked. Some of these politicians are so cruel that even when their wife is battling cancer, instead of standing by her, they go to bed with another woman and make babies. Shameful, isn't it?

I could not believe a politician, who should be a role model to the country, could cheat on his own family. How can somebody be dishonest and a cheater to his own family but not to other people? Role models should live up to moral standards—that's very important for the country. But the good thing is, no matter how hard they try to cover for their shameful acts, with the media these days they aren't able to. Not being able to trust the politicians is bad for America.

Another thing that really surprised me was having different parties, like the Democrats and Republicans, argue so harshly over little or big things. I was very disappointed because in my mind I believed in the name the *United* States of America. When I moved here, I realized people are not as united as the name of this country says.

While Americans argue so hard and try to make the opposite party look bad, other countries see this as an opportunity and give their best to try to get ahead of this great and superpower country. Parties don't make sense to me. I believe this is one country and it is time to put aside politics and start doing positive things for this country together.

Politicians get argumentative over anything and start picking on each other instead of spending their time and energy to solve the problems in this country. By arguing over small disputes, Americans forget the real and the big picture. I am afraid it will be too late by the time they wake up. Americans should honor the real meaning of the United States of America and stand united together, making this country greater than ever.

Is there a war going on between some news channels? They are unaware that they are damaging the reputation of America. Two news channels in particular make me wonder sometimes. With all the money, energy, and time they invest to hate or say bad things about each other, why can't they spend it to move this country in a constructive direction?

Having Obama elected as the president of the United States proved there is no cheating in America's elections, unlike some other countries. I believe President Obama has a lot on his plate and a lot to fix. I also know he can't do it on his own. America is great mostly because of its people. Every single person needs to do their share to help put an end to today's problems. If they can't help, at least they shouldn't do any harm. Americans need to get together to fix the long-term challenges instead of accusing each other's party.

My sons had never cared for politics before. It was surprising to me to see how much they followed the news and politics this last election as an African American became president of the United States.

CHARITY AND GENEROSITY

Americans are the most giving and generous people in the whole world. I like the fact that there is diversity in giving. I also like the fact that all kinds of people are involved with American charities. They not only help each other in time of disaster but also help other countries at times of earthquakes or other natural misfortunes.

OPPORTUNITIES

Not having enough opportunities leads to having limited chance for achievement. Hopefully this is not going on in America. People from all over the world give up anything to come to the United States in order to follow their dreams. I was so joyful to witness all kinds of opportunities available for all kinds of people of any ages; you can only witness this in America. There is a reason for calling America the land of opportunity.

I was surprised that people from other countries recognize the best use of America's opportunities, yet some Americans don't appreciate what they have. In America anybody can reach their dreams if they want to; this is impossible in most other countries.

Americans need to see and feel what they have been blessed with and appreciate and get the best use of opportunities in their own country. It made me wonder why some Americans don't use their own blessings and opportunities!

ADOPTING A CHILD

A lot of people turn to adoption to fulfill their dreams of family. I realize adoptive parents have abilities to love, care for, and raise a child; otherwise they wouldn't do it. Difficult laws are not fair to them nor to the adopted child. Children deserve and can use a loving and good home with wonderful parents.

I realized the fifty states have fifty different laws on adopting a child. I also realized that adopting in the United States is more like a business than about caring for the children. How sad. They need to change the system about adopting a child. Adopting a child doesn't mean buying or selling a child; it means loving a child from the heart and caring for a child financially. Why make it so difficult for something so pure and beautiful? Why make it so difficult for adoptive parents to give a loving home to thousands of kids who need a home?

I also realized that adoption in the United States costs a lot financially and emotionally. The adoptive parents, who want to share their love, home, and money with a child, end up with an empty bank account. To be able to raise a baby, parents need to have money. Let's at least have fair rules for the children.

CREDIT CARDS

That little piece of plastic really blew my mind. I had never seen a credit card before in my life. I was even more surprised when I found out about the use of it. How can people buy things with a little piece of plastic? How does it work? These questions came to my mind right away.

I applied for one and got it very quickly. I started to use it everywhere I went, from grocery stores to gas stations and restaurants. I made sure everybody saw it when I was using it. When I saw my friends, I took out my card from my bag and showed it to them. Some of them didn't have one, so I strongly recommended getting one. I told them how comfortable and happy I was with my credit card.

When I showed it to my sister, she said, "That's a piece of junk, and you are going to have a nervous breakdown when you receive your credit card bill."

I did not take her seriously and kept spending on my little piece of beautiful, shiny plastic. *This is so cool,* I said to myself every time I used it. I don't need to tell you how I felt when I received my first bill. Let me just say the bill was scary enough not to use the card anymore for a long time.

After a while I started to use it only when I had enough money in my bank account to pay my credit card bill. I learned from that mistake how to keep track of my available cash and my credit card spending.

As time went on, I became more and more aware and surprised of my findings about other people's spending on their credit cards. For instance, I realized American people spend money they don't even have or make on their credit cards. That adds up after a while and leaves them with no way out of debt.

The trick about credit cards is that when you use them, you don't feel like money is leaving you until you get that scary bill. But when you pay cash, you can feel the money is leaving you, and you can keep track of your money more easily.

I read that if you use credit cards instead of cash, you will spend 12 to 15 percent more—the ease of spending just entices you to keep going. I experienced the smartest way is to use only debit cards and cash.

The average family today carries $10,700.00 in credit card debt, according to the American Bankers Association. Seven out of ten Americans have credit card debt.

Be aware that you don't build wealth with credit cards. That's how the credit card companies have become multibillion-dollar companies. Get smart on spending your money. It's never too late to learn and change your financial lifestyle.

HARD WORKING AMERICANS

I was introduced to the owners on my first day of work at McDonald's. They were a very nice and friendly couple, but what amazed me was that they both were working and doing things we as employees were supposed to do.

When Dale, one of the owners, started to mop the lobby floor, I thought he was crazy. *What is he doing mopping the floor? Isn't he the boss?* I asked myself. It did not take long to find the answer to my question. When I saw my boss mopping the floor, I got encouraged and started to work harder.

He was also teaching the employees that mopping the floor or cleaning the tables won't hurt your character and personality. I realized that was his way to encourage the employees to work harder and better, without embarrassing them or hurting their feelings in front of the others. Later, when I became a manager, I did the same thing. It worked better than ordering the employees around. I learned the simplest and the nicest way to get my employees to work hard.

This is one of the things that make America a great superpower. When Americans work, they work hard. Americans are the hardest working people in the whole world.

SHOPPING CENTERS

I was very amazed and impressed to see the huge and beautiful shopping centers. All kinds of stores, from famous brand-name companies to small independent stores all gather in one gigantic area called a mall. I was pleased to see people from all different countries gathered for shopping in one place. I felt like the mall brought the whole world together.

The first mall I stopped by was the Galleria Mall in Houston, Texas. I went crazy; I was confused and overwhelmed. Was this a shopping center or a small city with different kinds of stores, banks, and restaurants? I was so confused and didn't know where to start looking. The floor was so clean and shiny.

For a while, I was drawn into my own world of observation. I went toward loud music coming from a big place. As soon as I opened the door, I could hardly see because of the smoke in the air and very low light. After two or three minutes, my eyes got used to the low light. There were lots of people plus a band and a singer. I stayed there for almost five minutes, and then went out to search the rest of the mall.

When I looked down from the second floor, I realized there was a huge ice-skating rink, with mostly young ice-skaters wearing cute clothing that was pleasantly beautiful. I went downstairs and watched every single beautiful move they were making; the way they were moving brought joy and peace to me.

I felt I wanted to explore and see everything at the same time at the mall. I walked everywhere that my legs could take me. I was amazed at the fancy and beautiful stores, the very well-designed shopping areas, the magnificent decoration, the relaxing sitting areas, and the beautiful clothes, shoes, and furniture.

CHILD PREDATORS

I had always thought of America as a peaceful, perfect country with right and protective laws, especially for its children. I was depressed and disappointed to realize there are many homegrown terrorists who kidnap little children, sexually molest them, and either kill them or keep them, yet the law is not harsh enough for these criminals. I became madly sad. A good and harsh enough law would prevent the crime, not increase it.

When I heard that a beautiful little girl was kidnapped, sexually abused, and buried alive by an old man, I became sick and still can't get it off my mind.

Perhaps the law is not harsh enough for child predators. Perhaps that's the reason for this growing problem. Perhaps there is a voice of encouragement for predators in the laws, making this crime grow instead of being stopped. I believe laws must be harsh enough to stop a crime from growing worse. Perhaps the voice of encouragement makes evil people do bad things more frequently.

What are the lawmakers thinking? What if something like this happened to their own little girl and family? Everybody knows a perfect law should put a stop on a crime or reduce it, not make it grow bigger—otherwise what's the purpose of the law? This is nonsense. Some lawmakers are hurting America and its innocent people and children, instead of helping them.

Child predators are evil, not sick. They should be punished as harshly as possible, but these laws show sympathy for their evil acts and call them sick. In most cases, they are sent to rehabilitation or set free under easy conditions.

What do you think? Do you think this is a sickness?

Newscasts have reported that one hundred thousand child predators are out there on the streets to hunt your children, and nobody knows where they are and what they do. They do it to your child, then go somewhere else and do it to other innocent children until they get caught and set free again to work on more evil plans against our innocent children.

What's the difference between a man who rapes and buries a little girl alive and a man who shoots and kills somebody in America? Why is the rapist or child killer considered a sick person who should get slight punishment, but the shooter goes to jail and gets harsh punishment? Why did the shooter get the punishment he deserved, but the rapist didn't? They both are sick minded, and both acts are evil. Don't you think the rapist should get more punishment for torturing and killing a little girl—or at least the same punishment?

I simply don't understand some of the laws in America, but I know one thing for sure: if the law against the rapist were harsh enough, the rapist disease would disappear because this is not a sickness; it's a crime and an evil act. Let's consider some facts, readily available when researching the Internet.

Sixty-seven percent of all sexual assault victims are under the age of eighteen.

More than half of all juvenile sexual assault victims are under the age of twelve.

One in four victims of sexual assault with an object are age five or younger.

Isn't it sad and dreadful? Doesn't this make you deeply angry? Doesn't this make you worry and concerned if you have a little boy or girl living at home? Where are the good laws to protect our children and America from home-grown evil and criminals?

I admire what Chris Hansen is doing. At least he is trying his best to give a wake-up call to parents and protect our children against the predators.

OLDER WOMEN CARE MORE ABOUT THEIR LOOKS

One thing that really amazed me was that middle-aged and older women care about and pay attention to themselves more than the younger ones. Where I came from, women forget about themselves, especially when they age; they think life is about the family and others. I noticed in the United States that most of the women look better and take better care of themselves as they age. They realize life is about them too as they grow older. The same women when they were young and going to college looked miserable and were tired most of the time. Women in America find themselves as they grow older.

FEMALE SEXUAL PREDATORS

It was surprisingly weird for me to realize there are sick female sexual predators that go after minor boys, especially at the places of education, middle schools and high schools. It's very shameful that a teacher, a trainer, a role model goes after children in educational places like schools.

SOME AMERICANS LIVE FOR OTHER PEOPLE

I realized that many Americans live for others instead of having a joyful life of their own. I witnessed that this group of people are never happy with what they have; they always search for the things they don't have, and this makes them not think about and enjoy the things they have.

When you don't have the money to spend but you keep spending, you live for others.

When you spend more than you make, you live for others.

When you spend or buy things to show off, you live for others.

When you don't learn how to say *no* to others, you live for others.

If you like to be happy and live for yourself, be grateful for what you have, not what you don't have.

If you like to be happy and live for yourself, don't think about what other people think of you as long as you do things in a right and honest way.

HOSPITAL MISTAKES

Unbelievable! Hospital mistakes kill about ninety-eight thousand people every year in the United States, according to FOX News. I still can't believe it!

MEN RESPECT WOMEN

I was shocked when I witnessed how some men treat their women in a very tender, loving, helpful, and respectful way. Some men sacrifice a lot to make sure their women have a good life or have free time to go shopping without children, go on a trip with their female friends, and a lot more. I witnessed that in some cases, the men go to work all day and the wife takes care of the children. As soon as the husband gets home, he has full responsibility for the children so the wife can do her own thing. That blew my mind!

PARENTING

This is not about the kids because they don't have any knowledge of anything—this is about parents. Even though sometimes there are exceptions, and some kids end up parenting their parents. The problems children end up having later in life start from the family and the way they were raised and then schooled. Parents need to connect with their children in an honest and direct way from an early age.

Children learn and understand better when they are little because their mind is so fresh and there are no worries, no madness, and no sadness. I mean nothing is bothering them at childhood, so they have the brain ability to grasp and learn things quickly. Our job as parents is to educate them as best we can and dump beautiful things into their innocent and pure minds. We need to teach and educate our children in a fun way because they learn better when they have fun. The things my parents taught me from the early age of three until I was ten years old, I have carried throughout all my life. They have had a huge impact in my life.

I remember I was about eight years old when I asked my mom for a glass of milk. She gave me half a glass of milk. I didn't want it. "This is half empty," I said.

"Look at the glass again and tell me what you see in it," she said.

I looked again and responded, "I see a half-empty glass of milk."

"Why, I see a half-full glass of milk," she said. Then she turned to me and said, "By the way, how can you see the emptiness in the glass but not the visible milk?" She always tried to teach me to see the positive side of everything.

As parents we need to be powerful role models and deal with our children with compassion, kindness, patience, gentleness, and knowledge.

Education is key not only for our children but also for us as parents. Don't think you know everything just because you are called parents. In order to educate our children in a right way, we must educate ourselves first and do things in a right way. Share your love with them and create a strong bond between you and your children.

Raising a child is a once-in-a-lifetime opportunity. Do it right because you are never going to get another chance. Sometimes I wish I could go back and get one more opportunity to raise my children. If I could get another chance, I would raise them differently from what I already did. We as parents can always do better.

I would tell them more often how much I love them, how much I need them, how much I care for them—if I were given another chance.

I would take my time more patiently to tell them I am sorry, thank you, please, forgive me, you are the best, the smartest, the kindest—if I could get another chance.

I would think twice and set selfishness aside and tell them, "I apologize, I was wrong, I would make it up to you, my angel."

If I had another opportunity to raise my kids, I would connect with them better, I would look into their lives and needs better, and I would take a break from seriousness and start having serious fun with them.

If I were given another chance, I would hold, hug, kiss, educate, and love them more, instead of being difficult, ignorant, pushy, and stubborn toward them. I would guide and assist them more instead of being unhelpful and cruel. I would make them feel more safe, secure, and welcome.

I would work much harder on establishing a strong relationship between God and my children so they won't be broken easily in times of problems.

It is still not too late. Every morning, life give us another opportunity to do things better. It's never too late to make something positive out of something negative. Always love your family, friends, and others like it's the last day of their lives. If I knew this would be the last minute that I would see my best friend, I would embrace, love, help her strongly. Isn't it better to be like this toward our family and loved ones all the time?

The most healing thing we can do for ourselves is to love, care, give, respect, share, understand, and forgive others as best we can. When you forgive, you set yourself free. You always forgive the person, not what they did.

When I was a little girl, I used to live in a city that was surrounded by very beautiful high mountains. We could see the mountains no matter where we lived or were. I would go to the front yard and look at the mountains from our house and wished to God that I could be on top of the mountains one day. When I grew older, we as a family started to go mountain climbing on the weekends. I realized that to get to the top of the mountain, I needed to climb the mountain first.

I could not reach the top the first three times; it wasn't easy, and I would climb back down very disappointed. I even remember asking God, "Why can't you just lift me and place me on the top to let me satisfy my childhood wish?" Sometimes I cried, screamed, feared, fell back a little on the way up. Sometimes I got tired to the point that I could hardly breathe. Many more emotional and physical challenges appeared in my way. Sometimes I got to a situation where I thought I would fall and die.

I will never forget the day that I reached the top. I felt joy and victory. I felt I had challenged the hard rocks and mountain and conquered. I learned one of the most valuable lessons of my life.

I learned I would love to be and live on the top of the mountain, but to get to the top, I first needed to climb the mountain and surmount a lot of problems on the way up. Children need to know that to get to the top and victory, there are some failures along the way. The most famous and important men in history are known because of their many failures. Nonetheless, they hit the ground and got back up; they kept going until they reached the top. Don't look at problems as problems; look at them as a way leading you to the victory. Look at them as a way to discover success.

The collection of mistakes and pains that happen in the years of your life are called experience. They will eventually lead you to success, and you will become more valuable. Every problem has a solution next to it, and every painful story can have a successful ending. As long as a problem has a solution next to it, there is no need to worry about it. If a problem can't be solved and it's out of our control, what's the use of worrying?

Children are born pure and innocent. Today's criminals weren't born criminals. Children are entitled to happiness, joy, and peace. If you fail dealing with your child, try a new way to deal with them. Kids are kind, flexible, and innocent. Don't get their brains stuck on any bad habit. Don't lose control of your kids. Keep close track of their friends. If you made a mistake, don't panic; it's never too late to start anew. We can't go back and change a bad mistake, so save your energy to start anew and create a successful plan. There are always better plans and opportunities in front of you. We need to recognize our mistakes first, instead of judging our children's mistakes.

Life salutes you when you make your family and others happy. Each of us has different dreams, talents, and destinations, but we all have the same power to start anew today. If we don't, today is going to be another day like yesterday.

Once in a while, have a meeting with your family and make them aware of the realities in life. Ask them if they need help. Tell them you need their help on saving electricity, water, and gas or cleaning the yard. Having a pet at home is going to make children responsible; by cleaning up after their pet, they will grow up as a caring and loving person. Children like to feel and be important. Give them a chance and make them feel special and proud. Make them feel they are part of the solution.

The three most valuable things in our and our children's lives are God, love, and self-confidence.

The most destroying things in human life are alcohol, pride, and anger.

The most important things in life that you should never give up on are God, hope, and honesty.

The most damaging things that can ruin our lives so easily are regret of yesterday, waste of today, and fear of tomorrow.

ABOUT GOD

When I was a little girl, I always thought God was sitting somewhere up there and watching every little move I was making. If I did anything bad, I kept begging him to forgive me because I was so afraid of him. My mom had told me you don't need to be scared of anybody but God. My thoughts about God changed as I grew older.

I realized that to have a relationship with God, we need to welcome him into our hearts. I realized God has unconditional understanding. I experienced God as very kind and forgiving and capable of anything. I realized his unlimited wisdom as I grew older. I completed my beliefs and trust in God's love, wisdom, integrity, and compassion. I keep my trust in him in all times, and I also call on him in truth. I have been in situations not knowing what to do, and I have been in situations out of my control. I prayed about it and realized God does answer our prayers. Most of our problems and situations can be changed through prayer. If things don't change, God has a better plan for you.

Count your blessings and write them down; then you will realize God is the greatest. Develop the power of your mind. Look at the sky, stars, our planet, and the other planets, and think about them. Look at the trees, flowers, water, rain, and snow, and think about them.

Look at yourself, inside and out. What are we? Why are we here? What's the purpose of life? What is life? What happens to us when we go to sleep? What happens to us when we die? Why do we have body and spirit? When we are alive, why do almost all people think more of their body than their spirit? When we die, why does our body go under the ground and our spirit go free?

Why are most countries and people fighting and waging war most of the time? Why do people kill and hurt each other? For what? Over what? Why do people hate and argue over every small thing? Why do some people cheat, lie, and steal to get a better house, car, furniture, and other fancy stuff? When the end comes, a very small box under the ground is going to be our house, and the only thing we take with us is our good deed or bad deed. Don't you have lots of unanswered questions? I do, and only God knows the answer to some questions.

I know one thing for sure: there is only one God, and he loves and helps the people who rely on his power and follow his rules. Things that are impossible to men are possible with God. God is for us. I take advantage of God in so many ways. He is my spiritual friend, my mental health, my happiness, my companion, and my understanding and forgiving friend. He is also my weight-maintenance friend. You probably wonder how. He exists for us any way we can get his help for a better life. He helps me to make healthy eating choices. I also use his help to exercise to avoid negativity and anger. If I have to do something and I don't feel like it, I make a quick promise to God. That promise makes me do it, because I wouldn't dare to break my promise with God.

If I haven't exercised one day and I am sitting on the couch watching TV and don't feel like getting up, a quick promise to God will send me out for a twenty-minute walk. I work at McDonald's, and I love their french fries. As soon as I walk in, I promise God I won't have any fries that day. That will take care of me staying away from fries. I love ice cream with chocolate topping. The temptation would kill me sometimes, but as soon as I make my promise to God not to have any, amazingly he even helps me to forget about it.

God has been so kind to me and my family, and I have a hundred percent belief in prayers. When I was younger and God answered my prayer, sometimes I thought it was an accident; but as I grew older, I started to believe in God and prayers more due to my experience. There have been times I prayed for something but it didn't happen. Something else against my will happened, but at the end good came out of it.

Prayers and doing our best have direct involvement in solving problems. Sometimes problems attack from everywhere at the same time. Don't panic! Write them down and put the list in your drawer. Six months later, look at it, and you will be surprised how most of them were solved by God's helping you. Leave the out-of-control problems to God.

I worship God in good times as well as bad times. He is on my mind most of the time, because everywhere I look I see a sign of him. God is great when nobody else wants to hear my sorrow, my stories, my talks, my happiness, my nagging, and my pain. He hears me and helps me to be in peace. He gives me hope when I feel nobody loves me. When I feel tired, he gives me strength. When I feel I am not able to solve my problems, he walks me through them.

When I am guilty and feel I can't forgive myself, he forgives me. When I feel stressed and upset, he says, "Leave it up to me." When I feel the loneliest, I know he is always there for me. You can use his help too. You just need to be a great believer in him. He is here for you.

By the way, I think life is a gift to us from God. I believe life is a mystery; it is a journey of love, friendship, passion, and gratitude. I believe that life is an adventure, movement, and freedom. Life is a purpose. Life is feelings, nature, and rain. And I believe that life is delightful and beautiful.

MY SURPRISES ABOUT DOGS

I hated dogs for many years. To me they were dangerous, nasty, and smelly. Come back with me to when I was only eight years old. I grew up in a family of eight, and everybody cared for animals. I always liked animals, but not their hair or smell. This made me stay away from them or be around them for a very short period of time. I remember my brother had a black cat, a turtle, a frog, and a rabbit. My sister always had little colorful hens. My mom always had a pair of lovebirds. I liked all of them a lot, but as I said, I did not like the hair, smell, and mess. Even though everybody took good care of their pets and kept them clean, there was still hair, smell, and mess.

Since I was a little girl, I have always been afraid of dogs. I didn't like their faces, especially when they showed their big, sharp teeth. It scared me to death. We moved to a house where our neighbors were Americans and they owned a huge scary dog. One day when I was standing by the door outside, a huge brownish dog started to run toward me. I was frozen and couldn't move. I thought the dog was going to kill me in a matter of seconds, but fortunately one of the Americans yelled at the dog and the dog ran back in their house. I thought the dog was going to kill and eat me. That was the first very frightening experience that I had with dogs. That experience was so bad it affected my relationship with dogs for many years to come. I felt sick for a while and had nightmares about dogs attacking me. Ever since then, I really hated dogs.

One day my dad bought a German shepherd and brought it home. That day looked like the last day of my life. I was so scared, upset, and worried. *Where did this nasty, scary, hairy, dangerous, smelly, and killer animal come from?* I asked myself. When I heard my dad telling my mom the dog was trained to attack anybody who came to the house, it scared the heck out of me.

In order for the dog not to attack or hurt my mom, my dad had to introduce the dog and my mom to each other. The first day my mom went out to the yard with my dad and the dog, I was very worried and scared that the dog might hurt my mom. I couldn't watch, so I went inside the closet and closed the door; I kept praying for my mom. "Please, God, don't let the dog attack my mom." I also covered my ears in order not to be able to hear anything. For several days my dad let my mom feed the dog while my dad was present too. After a while the dog got used to my mom, and he became friendly toward her.

There was a room, small kitchen, and small yard on the other side of the house, separated from the main building by a brick wall with a door in the middle. That became the dog's house. The dog was there all the time unless nobody was home or during the night. Then my dad would let the dog out in the yard to protect everybody and the house. My mom would take the dog to his house early the next morning before we got in the yard and went to school. Thankfully the dog was away from me, and there was no way he could kill and eat me. That was my childhood experience with dogs. Later I found out the reason my dad bought a dog was because he had lots of valuable things at home, so when nobody was home, it made my dad feel safe and secure with the dog being present.

The dog was very protective and very dangerous to strangers. My dad would buy cow liver and stomachs or other parts of cows and sheep, and then my mom would cook and make food for the dog. That was one more responsibility added to my mom's. Even the dog ate healthy. There wasn't any dog food for sale in the stores at that time. I never heard of such a thing as dog food for sale in stores until after I moved to the United States.

When I and my cousin or friends got together to play in the backyard, the dog barked madly from his house and knocked on the door most of the time. "This dog is a killer and very dangerous. Don't even get close to his house," I kept warning my friends. That's what I really thought about the dog. On weekends while my dad was training the dog and exercising him, I sat by the window and looked out. I thought the reason the dog didn't hurt my parents was because they were big and strong.

Several years passed. My older sister got sick and had to have a tonsillectomy. On the way to the hospital, she was crying and handed me some money, begging me to take good care of her pets while she was gone. Seeing her cry and care that much for her pets surprised me. I kept my promise and looked after her pets, which were a rabbit and several little chickens. I started to like them deeply, but I still had the same thoughts about the dog.

Even when my dad's first dog died, it didn't bother me at all. I was kind of happy that my mom didn't have to cook for the dog anymore. But it didn't take more than a week for my dad to buy another dog. I did not understand the real reason why my dad did that. Nowadays I know that losing a pet is very difficult for the owner, and to get over the grief inside they replace the pet quickly.

Ever since my dad brought the first dog home, he constantly had a dog, but he never had more than one dog at a time. I stayed cold toward and away from dogs until I came to the United States. I was surprised and disappointed to see lots of dogs everywhere. Everywhere I went, I could see dogs; people were walking them on the streets or playing with them in the parks. I also could see them in people's backyards and in their cars; almost every other house had dogs in the backyard.

I was shocked when I looked at people's house and saw dogs inside sitting at the windows looking out. *What is this—a city of dogs?* I asked myself. If I was invited somewhere, my first question was, "Do you have a dog?" If the answer was yes, I never stepped foot in the house. I thought people must be really nasty to keep dogs inside their houses. What a messy lifestyle Americans had. When I look back, I remember that at least when my dad had dogs, he always kept them in the yard or a doghouse.

I had to walk to an English school that was almost an hour and a half away from the apartment. One day I heard a very loud bark from my left on the way to the school. I didn't even have a chance to look. I just jumped off the curb in front of oncoming traffic to be away from the barking dog. When I looked back, the yard was fenced. I almost got killed that day, because there were cars coming toward me and they had to stop quickly. One car was so close to me that I was lucky I wasn't hit by it.

The driver got out of the car and asked if I was okay. I just nodded my head and went to the other side of the street to be away from the dog. I could hear my heart pounding so loudly, the dog almost gave me a heart attack. I still could hear his loud barks as I was walking away. *What are these animals good for? They are dangerous and stinky. And they must also be dumb to attack an innocent person,* I thought. After that day I became more scared of dogs; it didn't matter if they were kept fenced or not.

One day my English teacher brought a picture of a dog to the school and proudly showed it to everybody, saying, "This is my lovely and beautiful dog. I love her to death. My dog comes before my family." I took it as a joke and started to laugh, wondering why nobody else laughed. Years later I realized she was serious that day, and I was the one who acted like a fool.

For thirty-two years the relationship between dogs and me stayed the same. It had started when I was eight years old and continued until I turned forty and met my second husband. We dated for a while. He had no idea how I felt about dogs, and I had no idea he owned two dogs. The first time he invited me to his house, he came outside to accompany me in. First he opened the door, and then he was going to open the storm door. Suddenly two big dogs jumped behind the storm door. It scared the heck out of me. There was a bench nearby. I sat on it and said, "Let's sit outside; it's very nice out."

I was nervous and a little shaky, but tried to control my nerves. Those two ugly dogs were rubbing their faces, their noses, and their tongues on the storm door. I was almost going to vomit. *They couldn't be nastier than that,* I thought. *They can't wait to get out and hurt me.* I completely forgot I was on a date with their owner, Ali. I was so stressed and scared that he noticed and asked me if I was afraid of the dogs. I replied, "No, I care for them because they are God's creatures. I just don't like the smell, hair, stickiness, and their sharp teeth."

He introduced the dogs to me from the other side of the storm door. The black one was Dudley and he was the father; the brown one was Cosmo, his son. They were both shar-peis. When Ali said they were both very friendly, I looked at them and wondered how they could be friendly when they were both barking at me and showing their big sharp teeth. They were very ugly and scary, and I didn't like them at all. I thought any minute they might break the glass and attack me, so I said good-bye to my friend and released myself from there. I couldn't sleep most of the night. I had to break up with Ali because of the two dangerous dogs he owned and loved and I hated.

The next day he stopped by my workplace to see me. I tried to act normal, but I was cold inside because of his owning two dogs. There was no way I could put up with the dogs or even get close to them. I needed to talk to him so each of us could go our own way. On the other hand, he was so wonderful and not pushy about the dogs or anything else. This made me relax a little and reconsider my decision.

I went back to his place after two or three weeks on my own. He appeared on the other side of the storm door with the dogs on his sides, impatiently scratching the glass. All of a sudden he yelled at the dogs to sit. Amazingly they both moved away from the door and sat on the floor and did not move. Then he opened the door a little, said hi, and asked if I would like to go in and spend some time with the boys. *Did I heard him right? Did he call the dogs his boys? No, that's impossible,* I thought.

I thought maybe his grandsons were at his house, so I stepped in. I felt safe and secure that the dogs had listened to Ali. Plus he and his grandsons were there with me in case they attacked me. I stepped inside the house very cautiously, saying a prayer. As soon as I went in, they both ran toward me. One started to jump all over me, while the other one was cleaning his nasty nose on my pants. I had my eyes shut for a little moment so as not to see what was going to happen to me next. Again my friend yelled at them, and they moved away from me.

Ali suggested if I pet the boys a little, they would leave me alone, but I didn't want to touch them. "By the way, did you just call the dogs your boys?" I asked. Before he could respond, I said, "These are dogs, animals, not your boys." By then the dogs were all over me again, and my black pants looked very nasty and wet. I felt I needed to get out of there as quickly as I could. On the way home, I was preoccupied by his calling the dogs his boys. *What's wrong with him, calling the dogs his boys? He is weird,* I thought.

Several days later, he stopped by my job with one of the dogs in the backseat. He mentioned that one of the boys had been sick and he had to take him to the doctor. It was just so weird for me to hear the word boys instead of dogs. "You mean one of the dogs?" I asked. "What's wrong with the dog?"

"Cosmo hasn't been eating for a day and a half," he replied.

I went outside. Cosmo was in the backseat and looked sick, but as soon as he saw me, he started to wag his tail. I stuck my hand through the open window to give him some love and attention. Instead, he rubbed his wet, nasty nose against my hand and made it wet. I became very mad and rushed inside to wash my hands very quickly. While I was washing my hands, I kept muttering, "Those nasty dogs, nasty dogs."

The next day I stopped by Ali's house to see if Cosmo was doing better, and he was. I was surprised when I found myself inside the house and asking about him, but I had to leave very quickly because the dogs kept sniffing me and rubbing their noses on my clothes. I had to rush back home to change clothes. *They are so nasty,* I thought.

I started to care for the dogs a little without even noticing it myself, but I still didn't like lots of things about them. I didn't like them to get close to me; it took me about six months to get used to them. When Ali bought the dogs Christmas gifts, it was so weird for me. And the fact there were two gifts from the dogs to me was unbelievable!

To get to know the dogs, I had to face my fear and enter their world. I wanted to experience why they are so special to people. I couldn't stay away from my wonderful friends because of dogs. *I had to do something about it,* I thought. *As I make friends with people, I need to make friends with their dogs too.*

Finally Ali and I got married. The first thing I realized was that the dogs jumped on the bed and slept on it too. That was beyond my expectations. I could not stand it, and I needed to have some rules for them. I asked my husband if they could have their own bed. He agreed and we bought two beds for them, but we still needed to train them to sleep on their own beds. It didn't take long for them to quit jumping on our bed and start sleeping on theirs. I trained them myself. I felt like I had done something huge, and I realized there is a way to communicate with dogs.

I was very impressed with how smart and trainable they were. The dogs were also sneaky, because every little chance they had when we weren't around, they would get on the bed. This upset me. They were smarter than that because they didn't do it in our presence. For instance, if we were out and left the bedroom door open, they would have a delightful time; we could tell from the messy, unorganized sheets and covers. I had to wash and clean everything from the beginning. Every time they would do something bad while we were gone, as soon as we opened the door, they would go out through the doggy door and stay in the backyard until we calmed down. They knew they were going to get punished for their bad behavior.

The dad, Dudley, was very wise and patient, but Cosmo was very naughty and hyper. Both were very smart. One of the rules was they didn't get close and sniff me because I hated their wet noses and the smell of their mouths, especially when they were breathing with their mouths open. My husband gave me a flyswatter and told me, "In case the dogs get close to you, you can scare them away by waving the flyswatter in the air. It will make them stay away." The next time Cosmo got too close to me, I started to swing the flyswatter in his face; it worked and scared him away.

Several days later, after I made dinner, set the table, and started to eat, all of a sudden Dudley started to make unusual noises from down his throat. He vomited right next to the dinner table. That was the nastiest thing I had ever heard or seen or smelled. I ran to the bathroom and started to vomit too. I couldn't eat for a while because every time I was going to eat something, the picture of Dudley throwing up would pop up in front of my eyes and make me sick to my stomach.

My husband cleaned the backyard every day, picking up after the dogs. He also used Lysol to wash the patio, but I still could sense the bad smell. If I was walking through the backyard, I looked carefully in front of me every step I took to be sure I wouldn't step on their poop. Inside every corner of the house, I had beautiful candles and lots of air freshener. Still, the smell would bother me sometimes. Maybe the smell was just in my mind, because my husband kept saying he didn't smell anything.

Life with the dogs wasn't easy. If we were out somewhere, as soon as we got home they were at the door waiting and jumping on us. I always sent my husband in first so they wouldn't jump on me, but they would do it most of the time regardless. I found out that when I blew in their faces, it would keep them away from me, so when the flyswatter wasn't around that was a good trick to use to keep them away.

The house had four bedrooms, and the dogs were allowed to walk through all the rooms except mine. I made sure the door was shut all the time. One day when I got home from work, I realized my husband had left the door open. That gave the dogs an opportunity to get into my personal stuff. They had torn up some pictures, which really made me angry. This happened several times. *They have the whole house to themselves, and I can't have only one room to myself,* I thought.

Finally I had enough of their smell, hair, and mess. I asked my husband if we could keep them in the backyard. "They are short-haired dogs. The heat in the summer and the cold in the winter will affect them and make them ill," he protested. That was another dead end. I was also jealous about the dogs and kept nagging my husband, "You care for them more, you pay attention to them more, and you spend your money on them more." My husband was nicer than to say anything. He began paying more attention to me, although he still had the same routine with the dogs. By then I knew the dogs weren't dangerous; the problem was there were things about them that I didn't like at all. For instance, when they were shaking, I could see nasty stuff coming out of their noses and mouths all over the walls and the furniture. We had to clean often.

Every evening if I was home, we would take the dogs out for their walk. If I wasn't home, my husband would take them by himself. I noticed my husband would take two plastic bags and two rubber gloves with him every time we were going for a walk. When I asked him the reason, he said that in case the dogs pooped, he would pick it up in order to keep the neighborhood clean. *How embarrassing it would be for him to pick up the poop,* I thought. (Later in life I realized it would be embarrassing if we didn't clean up after our dog messes.) I thought he was joking about picking up the poop, but the first time we took them for a walk and the dogs pooped, my husband stopped to clean it up. I was too embarrassed and just kept walking away, not even looking back.

The next time when he was going to take the dogs for a walk and asked me to go, I refused. I told him, "You embarrass me by picking up the poop." He and the dogs went for a walk, and I stayed home. This went on for almost a month until I convinced myself that he was doing something healthy for the neighborhood and there was no reason for me to be mad. I started to pay attention to other people to see if they picked up after their dogs' messes. I noticed most of them did not clean the mess. By then I realized my husband was doing a good thing. I think everybody should do that to keep the parks and streets clean, just like their own backyard.

After three years we moved to a new house. It was a lovely house. We bought everything new from the beginning and got rid of the old furniture. The rugs we bought were very beautiful, handmade in Pakistan. I was so afraid the dogs would get close to the furniture and shake themselves, leaving nasty spots on our beautiful new furniture. I started having new rules for the dogs at the new house. Since the house was a two-story house, I asked my husband if the dogs could stay downstairs and we stay upstairs. He agreed.

The first day that we moved to the new house, the dogs were acting crazy and out of control. The first thing I did was to block their way to the upstairs. My husband tried to show and teach them to use their new doggy door. I went downstairs and tried to help him. Finally, after almost an hour of trying hard, they learned how to go through the doggy door. We went upstairs to rest a little. After a while I went downstairs to check on them. I realized they had pooped and peed all over my beautiful rugs. I can still feel how mad and upset I got over what they did and the terrible smell. I started to cry. I cried until I went to sleep that night.

Poor Ali was very stressed out; he was also very patient. I learned a lot along the way from Ali because of how wonderful he was. The next day I woke up early in the morning to go downstairs to make sure the dogs went out to do their thing. As soon as I stepped down, I noticed they had pooped and peed all over the rugs again. I sat on the floor and started to cry again. Amazingly the dogs sat in front of me sadly and started looking at me. After a while I felt the dogs were crying with me. I could see the tears in their eyes.

They were trained to stay away from me, but when they saw me crying, they came close to me. I felt they could feel my pain and they were trying to comfort me. At that moment I felt there was more to them than I knew. For the first time I felt some peace about them in my heart. I woke my husband up and helped him wash the carpet. I asked Ali to buy a gate and separate the downstairs from the upstairs. We kept them downstairs all the time. The doggy door was downstairs too, so they could go out and play in the backyard. But they wouldn't go anywhere; instead, they stayed by the gate the whole time and made all kinds of noises.

My husband said, "The dogs like to be with us, that's the reason they are crying."

I felt bad, went downstairs, and opened the gate for them. They rushed upstairs without any hesitation. My husband was very surprised and said we shouldn't open the gate if we wanted them to stay downstairs, because they needed to get used to it. I said, "Let them stay upstairs while we are at home. When nobody is home, we can keep them downstairs."

The dogs were so happy to be around us. I started to think that these animals have a sense of kindness and emotions; they are also very protective of their owners. I just had never paid that much attention to know them better— now was my chance. I realized they listened to me too, especially when I wasn't in a mood to have them around. If I said, "Go lie down," they would hear and listen. I felt joyful and powerful that the dogs would understand and listen to me. Surprisingly, the dogs were happy if I was happy; if I was sad, they would sit in a corner of the room and look depressed. I started to understand and feel their presence more. I became more comfortable with them and made more time to spend with them. I would play with them and give them more attention. The dogs loved it when I rubbed their ears.

Winter arrived, and the weather got really cold. The dogs were trained to sleep downstairs in their own beds, but the fireplace was upstairs. The dogs loved the fireplace and as soon as we started to turn it on, they quit going downstairs to their beds. Instead, they slept right in front of the fireplace at night and wouldn't go anywhere else. We had to take their beds to the living room every night in front of the fireplace, then take them downstairs every morning after they were awake.

Sometimes they would come to our bedroom and spend the night at our bedside. They snored sometimes, and my husband would kick them out of the bedroom in the middle of the night and shut the door behind them. When I confronted him, he said he did it for me so the dogs would not wake me up or keep me awake. "It's fine with me. Their snoring doesn't bother me. Let the boys be comfortable," I said. I couldn't believe that I had started to call the dogs boys myself.

Cosmo and Dudley started to come to me for more attention rather than going to my husband. Every time they were playful, they would come to me. If I ran, they ran after me; then I ran faster and laughed loudly like a little girl. Most of the time they kept me and my mind busy and entertained me; I never got bored when I was around them. Sometimes I laughed just looking at them. I never got bored when I was alone at home; I felt like someone was home beside me, and this made me feel safe and secure. They were lovable, funny, caring, and protective. I started to realize the importance of dogs.

By then I could see more good in them than hair, shakes, and danger. But still I would ask my husband to take them downstairs and close the gate when we both were leaving the house, because as I said, all the furniture was new. Also, I caught Dudley one day on the couch licking himself; it made me uncomfortable and mad. One day when we came home, Cosmo had some scratches and an injury on his head. When we took him to the vet, he said that Cosmo and Dudley had gotten into a fight. When we left the house the next time, we kept Cosmo upstairs and Dudley downstairs and locked the gate. We decided to keep them separated so they wouldn't get into a fight again.

First, let me tell you something nice about the dogs. When the dogs and I were at home and my husband was out somewhere, as soon as the dogs heard the garage door, no matter where they were or what they were doing, they rushed to the garage door. They started to bark and wag their tails. They couldn't wait for Ali to open the garage door and give them love and attention. I was surprised at the love and passion dogs have for their owners.

Anyway, as I said, we separated the dogs and left the house. When we got home, Cosmo wasn't at the door waiting for us. We started to look around, and we were shocked when we found him downstairs with Dudley. To this day we still don't know how he got downstairs with that tall gate in the way. My husband and I just kept looking at each other and asking how in the world he got downstairs. We checked the lock of the gate. It wasn't broken. The gate was both strong and tall. Cosmo was downstairs next to his dad, but nothing had moved or broken. We realized they didn't like to be apart, so we never separated them again.

I usually walked Cosmo and my husband walked Dudley whenever we went for a walk. I had to hold onto Cosmo very tightly because if he suspected a moving cat or rabbit or squirrel, he responded very strongly and tried to run from my hands. He was stronger than I, and sometimes he dragged me after him and the other animal too.

If either Cosmo or Dudley pooped, Ali was the one who always picked up after them. One day we made a bet while we were walking the boys. I bet on Cosmo not pooping while we were walking him. "Cosmo is definitely going to poop," Ali said. The bet was if Cosmo pooped, I was the loser and had to clean up after him—not just today but on all our future walks. If not, my husband was the loser and he had to continue picking up both Dudley's and Cosmo's poop. I was very sure Cosmo wasn't going to poop because I had seen him thirty minutes earlier do his business in the backyard.

My husband kept insisting Cosmo was going to poop and I kept insisting he was not. If I lost, I would be the real loser because that would be the first time for me to pick up poop and Ali was kind of used to it. On the other hand, I was pretty sure Cosmo wasn't going to do it. As we kept walking, Ali tried to talk Cosmo into pooping. I was a hundred percent sure he wasn't going to do it, so I saved my energy most of the way and kept making fun of Ali. Every time Cosmo stopped, Ali said he was going to do it. "No, he is not," I said. Dudley did his business, and my husband picked it up. I started to laugh at him. Ali said it was very soon going to be my turn and he would be laughing at me. We were getting close to the house, and I was glad Cosmo hadn't done his nasty business.

My husband was getting a little disappointed that he wouldn't be able to stand there and watch me dig my hand into Cosmo's poop, but he kept saying, "We are not home yet, and Cosmo is going to do it." I just kept laughing at him because we were almost home; it was only a few steps away. I was so happy because there was no way I could stand the smell and the poop. Finally we got to our neighbor's lot. Suddenly Cosmo stopped on their lot and started to do his business. I was shocked and couldn't keep my eyes off him because he had done his business earlier.

Anyway, I had to keep my bet and my word. I used to never even look when my husband was picking up after the dogs; if they did their business, I just kept going and left Ali and the dogs alone. Now I had to do it myself. Ali realized how uncomfortable I was, so he suggested he would do it instead. "No, it's okay; I can do it," I said. Then he handed me a rubber glove and a plastic bag and told me how to grab it. First I went several steps away to get some clean fresh air in my lungs, then I started to clean it. It was disgusting— even my eyes were burning from the nasty smell. That was my first experience of pooper scooping.

I started to feel that the dogs had a positive effect on me. They also helped me grow out of my box and be able to see the real world of dogs. Eventually I felt like they were part of the family, and I liked and cared for them just as they did for me. I still kept them downstairs when nobody was home, and they hated it. I had come a long way to give myself and the boys a chance to know each other.

If I sat somewhere quietly, they would sit in front of me to find out what was wrong with me. With them around, I had to laugh and be happy all the time; otherwise I would witness two sad faces right in front of me. Months went by, and we were becoming more like a family.

One day when we were in the living room watching TV, Dudley caught my attention. I noticed he kept sniffing Cosmo's side. I thought he was just showing his fatherly love, so my attention went back to TV again. The next day while eating breakfast, I saw Dudley sniffing Cosmo's side again. This time I asked my husband, "Why is Dudley sniffing Cosmo's side?"

Ali said, "They do that to each other sometimes."

I didn't know why my inside feelings weren't good about this matter. The next time when I saw Dudley push on Cosmo's back with his chin, make Cosmo lie down, and then start to sniff and lick Cosmo's side, it made me worry. I told my husband, "I think Cosmo has lost some weight."

Ali said, "It's possible, but he eats normally so there is nothing to worry about."

I didn't mention anything else to my husband until Dudley kept sniffing Cosmo's side several more times.

By then I had spent several years with them, and I had never seen them acting like this. *It was something new they were doing and there must be a reason for it,* I thought. Dudley wasn't as happy as he used to be; he was trying to care for his son more than usual. I became sure something was going wrong between the dogs and something was bothering Dudley.

One night when I was still awake, I noticed Dudley come to my husband's bedside. He just stood there and kept looking at Ali. "Go back to your bed," Ali told Dudley.

Dudley walked out of the bedroom and went to the living room in front of the fireplace. I got out of the bed and followed him quietly. A terrible electric feeling came to me when I saw Dudley sniffing on Cosmo's side and licking the same place. I went back to my bed thinking, *What can be wrong?* The next day, I told my husband something was wrong with Cosmo and I thought Dudley knew what it was. "I think Dudley has been trying to give us a message," I said. At the same time that we were talking, I saw Dudley try to push Cosmo down, then he started to sniff and lick Cosmo's side.

I once heard that a lady was rescued by her dog from cancer because her dog kept sniffing on a particular area. The lady went to the doctor and found out she had cancer in the same area her dog was sniffing. "I know that dogs have the power to notice cancerous areas, but I just didn't take it seriously," I told Ali.

The same day we took Cosmo to his vet. They did an X-ray on his stomach. We got the result after waiting for a while. We found out Cosmo did have stomach cancer. When I heard the word cancer from the vet, I entered my own world shocked and amazed. *Animals know better than humans,* I thought. I had never seen or experienced such a beautiful thing between animals until then. Dudley was trying to get our attention all this time, and the poor dog was being ignored by us. He was trying his best to show us something was wrong with his son. He was begging us with his actions and eyes to save or do something for his baby, but he was ignored instead.

I couldn't even imagine what suffering he was going through. It gave me tears when I looked back and realized the reason he couldn't sleep at nights and kept coming to our bedside. *Poor Dudley, if he could just talk, it wouldn't have been any problem.*

My mom used to say, "Actions speak louder than words," but I always thought this was right only about humans. I now experienced this was more right about animals, because that's the only language they are able to use to communicate. Everything I was experiencing about the dogs was unbelievable for me; it was beautiful and pure, and I realized they know better than we do—they just can't use words.

The veterinarian prescribed some pills for Cosmo and told us after ten days of taking the pills, he needed to go back for surgery, a surgery that the doctor wasn't very hopeful about. But we needed to do our best to save him for his dad, especially since his dad had already gone through a lot. When we got home that day, Dudley was waiting at the door impatiently. I felt he was confused for a while, and then he started sniffing and kissing his precious son. Dudley seemed to be well aware of what was going on in his son's body.

My husband and I were very upset. I wished I had never known or had the boys, and then I would be free of suffering. Now I was worried about Cosmo having cancer and more sad and worried about Dudley witnessing his son's pain and probable death. To me it looked like Dudley was in more pain than Cosmo was. The first thing I did was to get rid of the gate between upstairs and downstairs. I felt guilty and was full of regret.

I could hear my husband's weeping. He and the dogs had been together since the dogs were puppies; it was very hard on him. Dudley was trying to spend more time with his son, knowing he wouldn't be around that much longer. His reaction toward Cosmo was so moving and heartbreaking. They had their own separate beds, but Dudley slept close to his son those nights. Cosmo was getting weak very fast, even though he was under good care and taking his medications regularly. I could feel and see a great deal of pain on Dudley's face and eyes. Sometimes I tried to distract him from his grief, but it never worked for long. Cosmo held his full attention. Dudley was worried and depressed. Cosmo was dying. I could see fear in my husband's eyes, and I was lost.

Dudley tried to control all of Cosmo's moves. He was also nervous. For instance, he would follow his son all the time. When Cosmo was walking, he would place his chin on Cosmo's back and push down until Cosmo lay down. Then he gently started to lick and kiss the cancerous area. How he knew about the cancerous area was unknown to me.

Those days sometimes when I was watching them, I thought about how, instead of talking, what if I had the dog's power of knowing what was going on inside everybody's body? The good thing was that the dogs had this unbelievable power. The bad thing was that most people don't pay attention to their unusual and out-of-the-ordinary moves until it is too late. I started to have a hundred percent trust in Dudley. He knew his son was going to die, and that was so painful. I couldn't leave my husband and two sad dogs at home with a terrible situation, so I decided to take off work for two weeks and bring some joy to the situation. From Dudley's acts, I knew Cosmo was in the last days of his life.

I decided to make those days a little easier on everybody. I got off work for a while and stayed home. To me Cosmo was going downhill very fast. Dudley sat by his side all the time. Whenever Cosmo lifted his head, he saw his dad there. Cosmo eventually stopped eating little by little, but I was glad he was still drinking. I knew that would come to the end very soon too, because the message was loud and clear.

When I witnessed the discomforting look in Cosmo's eyes, it ripped my heart. He used to never blink, or if he did, it was so quick that I couldn't notice; now his blinking was heavy and slow. He couldn't go to sleep most times at night, so he slowly walked to our bedside to get some attention. Then I crawled off the bed, followed him to the living room, gathered him up on my lap, and gently rubbed his ears and sang for him, thinking he might go to sleep. I prayed God to keep him away from pain. I also prayed for Dudley to be patient and away from grief.

By then I could completely understand Dudley's language and the things he was asking us to do for his son. He could make his thoughts known to me. Somehow he was communicating with me in many ways. Maybe he had always been like this, but I just never paid close attention to him. Now every move he made, it meant something to me. Sometimes when I had Cosmo on my lap, I thought back and felt so much regret about my behavior toward them that my heart was squeezed badly. I needed to go to a desert with nobody around, to scream and cry so nobody could hear me but God. We as humans don't appreciate what we have until the time of losing them. Then they become important to us—too late.

I realized there were moments we lived in but didn't feel the love and joy of those moments. When time had passed and we looked back, we could realize how precious and joyful those moments were. Enjoy the present and the moments you live in. I used this experience and decided to make the present moments as joyful as possible for them and me, so in the future when I looked back, instead of feeling regret, I could enjoy those moments. There were also moments between me and the boys that made me suffer and regret; I needed to fix those moments for my own sake.

Life is beautiful as long as we make the best of it. What Dudley was doing was the real meaning of pure love toward his son. I was ashamed of my previous behavior toward them. Those days I had plenty of time to look back and think about the years that I had missed loving animals. I looked far back to the year when I was only eight. I thought maybe that trained dog was running toward me only for love and affection. I always thought I was a caring and loving person, but watching these pets, I realized I still have a long way to go. That dog had taught me as much about love as anybody else.

I was caught in the moment with those dogs by observing their terrific love affair with each other. The charming relationship they had together in the moments of needing each other gave me an odd feeling. It wasn't hard for me to fall for another human being, but I couldn't believe I was hurting so badly because of those dogs, the animals that I used to hate.

What interested me most and caused my attention toward the dogs was the way they were behaving toward each other. I was witnessing human qualities or even more than that in them. When I looked back, I realized how hard Cosmo was trying for my happiness when he was well and cancer free. That unleashed emotions in me. I regretted that I didn't live in those moments to feel the pure love and real happiness they were offering me. On the other hand, how little I did for him in his healthy days and how much he did for me. I had to make it up to him; otherwise I would suffer forever.

I looked back and realized how careless and mean I was toward them and how careful and kind they were toward me. I looked back and realized how impatient and aggressive I'd been and how patient and grateful they had been. I looked back and realized how I knew nothing about those creatures; the only thing positioned in my mind was they were dangerous, nasty, hairy, and smelly. All these thoughts were eating me and making me be a better person and do my best to please them during Cosmo's last days of life.

Those dogs knew how to speak with me; I started to understand them better by communicating with them better. My dad used to say, "If you don't know how much you know, learn more. The more you learn, the more you realize how much you don't know." My dad was right: the more I was learning about these dogs, the more I was finding out how unknowledgeable I was about them. That was a big mistake I made for many years, blocking my mind against learning more about dogs.

If you block your mind about something or some kind of animal or other people and be hateful about their color, their religion, or where they come from, get close to them and learn more about them. You will be surprised how you change your mind toward them. I was the one who was hurt for being so hateful toward dogs for many years. I was the one who missed spending time with and the enjoyment of having them, and so I was the real loser.

The biggest problem with making a mistake is we don't acknowledge and correct it. It's never too late to accept the mistake and use the experience in the process of growing and learning. I was in that stage with dogs. Every moment I was observing and learning something very beautiful about them. Nasty, smelly, dangerous, and hairy had absolutely no more place in my mind. Instead, my mind was occupied with beautiful, caring, loving, smart, and protective boys.

My bond with and beliefs about dogs was getting deeper and stronger, especially since Dudley discovered his son's cancerous area. Dudley knew how to approach his son with warmth and shower him with love and attention. Sometimes Dudley would sniff the cancerous area heavily; it made me think Cosmo might be uncomfortable and stressed out over his dad's being overprotective. Sometimes I tried to get Dudley away from Cosmo so he could relax, get rested, and be in his own moments. We watched them almost all the time and made sure neither of them were hurt.

It amazed me how Dudley was trying to reach out to Cosmo and be around him all the time. In this matter Dudley had his own way of taking care of Cosmo. Every chance we weren't around, he went right up to his baby because in his innocent mind, he knew his child needed reassurance. The whole time, I never witnessed Cosmo going to Dudley.

I had my moments set around Cosmo more and my husband had Dudley. I was in their moments, and every single move they made it meant something to me. Dudley's strong reaction toward Cosmo made me believe Cosmo was going to go away very soon. It was in those moments that I realized dogs have a beautiful, innocent, and pure mind of their own. I wished I had known those beautiful creatures long ago.

I felt heartbroken about Dudley and started to pay attention and talk to him more. I petted Dudley every chance I got; it seemed petting him really relaxed him. Cosmo could hardly wag his tail a little, and he would rather come to my arms all the time. The day for surgery was getting closer, and Cosmo was getting weaker. On the other hand, Dudley's reaction toward his son was getting stronger. He gathered all his abilities to love, care for, and be around his son; he didn't want to waste any moments.

I was so sad about what the boys were going through, but I also was happy I took off work to be with them. The lessons I was getting from them were priceless. They fulfilled my moments with the loving relationships between them. They were like a teacher and I was their student, because I was learning the most valuable lessons about and from them. I felt if animals were that affectionate and caring, we as humans should be much better, but are we? They were also helping me to become a better human being, teaching me how to have consistent and clear communication with my family and friends.

I was learning there is an unbelievable lack of conflict in these animals. I was learning how to be obsessed with the positives, even in difficult times, and be able to give more. Just imagine what our world would be like if we contributed more purity and love, instead of conflict and negativity. When I looked back to the days we were taking the boys for a walk, I remembered they made the best of every walk. Every time we fed them, they ate with such enjoyment like it was their first meal. Every time we petted them, they wagged their tails and showed their love back to us like it was their first petting.

Dudley and his son had their own disagreements. Sometimes they barked at each other with anger, but they never took it to heart; the next minute they were sniffing each other and playing and moving forward. They celebrated and made the best of every walk, meal, moment, petting, and a whole lot more. I was learning how to live in the moment and get the best of my life and celebrate life every chance I got, because God had created everything good for us to be happy and grateful. The more I was getting to know the boys, the more I became embarrassed because of my past thoughts and behaviors toward them—but there was no time to waste on regret. I needed to make sure the boys were well taken care of during the toughest time and the grief they were in.

I realized these creatures contribute a lot to us. They put their lives in danger to protect us, they entertain us in many ways, they are our best friend and companion when we don't have a real one, they listen and do whatever we tell them to, they show us how to love and care for our family, friends, and loved ones. They are super faithful, they help the handicapped, they herd cattle and sheep, and they help the army and military. Dogs are used in prisons, police departments, airports, hospitals, and lots of other places. They help police find criminals and drug dealers. They heal children and adults. They relax you and bring your blood pressure down. They help you in hunting and lots of other things that they do for each other and us. Amazingly they do all this for us in exchange for just a little love and attention. They do all these things to see their owner happy and smiley.

Cosmo eventually lost his appetite for water too. He got so thin and weak to the point that he could hardly stand on his feet and I could see his bones clearly. I still remember the night before his surgery very clearly because it was super heartbreaking. None of us went to sleep that night; there was a sad silence in the air. I could see the pain and grief in Dudley's eyes; he stood by his son's side the whole night.

Cosmo came to our bedside several times. I had a feeling he was trying to pay his last visits to us. I felt so heartbroken and helpless; I couldn't avoid my tears that were coming down once in a while. Every time Cosmo stopped by our bed, I could hear my husband crying quietly. I got off the bed around two in the morning and went to the living room to spend time with Cosmo and Dudley and try to relax them. Cosmo slept on my lap and Dudley lay next to him. I felt a little better that everything was going smoothly. I sat with them until six in the morning.

We had to be at the vet's office by seven in the morning, so I had to get ready. When we were taking Cosmo to the car, Dudley stood by the door very sad and disappointed. He sniffed Cosmo several times and licked him a little. It seemed he was saying good-bye to his precious son.

Cosmo could hardly stand on his feet on the way to the hospital; instead, he lay on the backseat. At the hospital the nurse took control of everything and asked us to leave. The nurse said if something happened, she would give us a call. I had a strong feeling that I wouldn't be able to see Cosmo again, so I gave him a good-bye kiss and a hug.

My husband didn't kiss or hug Cosmo good-bye; instead, he told Cosmo to be a good boy. I realized he had not given up his hope for Cosmo. That scared me a little, thinking if Cosmo died, Ali would be truly hurt. I sent a prayer for Cosmo and hoped the best for him. We sat around for a while and then headed home, knowing Dudley was by himself and worried about his son. Dudley was standing by the door when we got home. We didn't have any sleep the night before, so I asked Ali to get some sleep in the bedroom. I went to the living room to be with Dudley.

Three hours later, the phone rang. My husband answered, and it was Cosmo's doctor saying something that made Ali cry. Ali could hardly talk, so I grabbed the phone. After they opened Cosmo's stomach for surgery, they realized the cancer had spread so badly; even if they went ahead and put him back together, Cosmo wouldn't live more than two weeks, and he would suffer great pain. They were asking for our decision quickly. Since my husband was so upset, I asked if I could call them back in a short moment after I talked to my husband. After I talked to Ali, we decided to let Cosmo go peacefully, without more suffering and pain, especially since he had gone through so much. This was the end of the journey for Cosmo.

I thanked God for giving me another chance to make it up to the boys. We were afraid Dudley might get depressed and sick after losing Cosmo, so Ali and I started to pay more attention to Dudley. My husband especially spent more time with him while I was at work. Surprisingly Dudley held his head high and didn't get sick or depressed.

I learned the biggest lesson of my life from Dudley before and after his son's death. When Cosmo was alive, Dudley was there and helpful for his son all the time, especially in the time of need. When Cosmo was gone, Dudley's worries were gone and he was back to his normal life. He had no regrets or worries because he did his best for his son. He didn't want to destroy his present and future by looking back to the yesterday. I was so impressed that I wrote a song about yesterday, today, and tomorrow. I named the song "Today."

Yesterday is gone, yesterday is gone,
Don't think about yesterday.
Tomorrow will come, tomorrow will come,
Don't think about tomorrow.
Today is here, today is fun.
Think about today, think about fun.
Yesterday is gone, tomorrow will come.
Today is here, today is fun.
Today is sweet, today is sad.
Today is down, today is up.
Today is here, today is fun.
Think about today, think about fun.
Yesterday is gone, tomorrow will come.
Today is here, today is fun.

KAMRAN'S MISSING DOG NAMED MAX

It was Tuesday, June 2, 2009. I had the day off from work. As you know, we women do more on our days off work—grocery shopping, cooking, cleaning, walking the dogs, washing, writing, calling family and friends, spending time with family, and a lot more. My middle son, Kamran, and his dog, Max, lived together with my youngest son, Sean, at the time.

As the day was falling deeper into evening, my husband and I sat on the couch exhausted. We decided to eat out at Carlos O'Kelly's, which was close to the kids' house, and then stop by to visit Sean and Max. Kamran was at work. I usually visited them an hour or two every day, but that day due to my heavy schedule I didn't.

Dinner at the restaurant was good. We headed to the kids' house. As soon as we got there, I noticed the back door was open. All of a sudden an electric feeling ran through my veins. I stepped inside the house and saw Sean coming toward me, looking very worried. I did not even ask what was wrong because I could feel it. "Mom, Max is gone," Sean said.

My whole world collapsed. I didn't even wait for an answer after I asked, "Where, when, how?" I ran outside and told my husband. He rushed back to his car and drove off looking for Max. The backyard was huge, with lots of trees, bushes, and corners. It had a pool in the middle, which was Max's favorite place. I was hoping he was hiding somewhere in the yard.

I started to search the backyard. It was raining. I sent Sean to the neighbor's to ask if they had seen Max. I knew the neighbor since the kids were living there. Her name was Clara, and she was a very nice lady. As soon as Clara found out Max was missing, she jumped in her car and started to look for him. There was no luck in the backyard. Sean and I thought we would split up and look carefully around the neighborhood, hoping Max might be hiding nearby.

I was still in shock, running and yelling Max's name. My tears were coming down, but thankfully the rain washed them away quickly. I couldn't believe he was gone. In the meantime, since God was the center of my world, I kept asking God for Max's safe return. I realized I should stop crying because if Sean saw my red eyes, he would feel guilty and become more upset. Sean and I got together with no results after thirty minutes.

"He must have gone to the streets," Sean said, so we jumped in Sean's car and started to search the streets close by. The more we drove around, the more we became disappointed, especially since it was dark by then. There was no sign of him; he was gone and had left us heartbroken. When we got home, neither my husband nor Clara was back yet. To me that was a disappointing sign because if they had located Max, they would already be there waiting for us. They must still be looking.

The stress inside me was taking away my energy little by little. I could see the signs of worry and guilt in Sean's eyes. I tried to comfort him by saying, "Don't worry, we will find him." It was so dark and still raining when first my husband and then Clara arrived empty-handed. We stood in the parking lot, thinking Max might come out of somewhere, but there was no sign of hope. I knew if I opened my mouth to say something, I would start crying, so I kept quiet until Clara got close to me and said how sorry she was for Max's disappearance. I needed to thank her for all she had done, but as soon as I opened my mouth, I started to cry. Sean and my husband then started to cry, and Clara's tears also streamed down.

There was a strong bond between Max and Clara. Every time Clara was working in the yard, Max looked out the window and then just waited at the door to get an opportunity to get out of the house to run to Clara's for some kisses. He wouldn't leave Clara alone until somebody went and carried him in. We thought that was funny and called them boyfriend and girlfriend. Sometimes I would go to the kids' house and see Max looking out the window while Clara was working in the front yard. I would say to him, "What are you doing by the window? Looking at your girlfriend? You want to go get some kisses?" As soon as he heard "kisses," his eyes got wider and he ran toward the door waiting for me to open it.

Clara left with tears in her eyes. The back door was still open for Max in case of his return. We sat in the living room. Worry, guilt, and fear was in all of our eyes. Nobody said anything; everything had happened very quickly. Sean thanked us and suggested we go home and get rested. He was alone and very upset, so we stayed. "Maybe Max will come back," I said. I didn't want to leave him alone. All of a sudden, the doorbell rang. We all rushed toward the door at the same time, hoping someone might have found Max and brought him back.

We were wrong; it was one of Sean's friends. She was surprised to see all three of us upset and at the door at the same time. I had absolutely no energy left; I couldn't even put a dead smile on my face. We left to search around more, knowing that Sean wasn't alone anymore. Everywhere we looked, there was no sign of hope. We headed home empty-handed.

Dudley, our dog, was waiting at the door for us. I patted his back and told him his grandson Max was gone. Dudley was a thirteen-year-old shar-pei, and Max was a fifteen-month-old French bulldog. I always saw Max as Dudley's grandson even though they had met only a few times by then. Max belonged to Kamran, my middle son. Due to Kamran's heavy schedule, Sean was the one who looked after Max mostly.

We got home around ten at night. I called my older son, Bob, and told him about Max. He got upset because he loved Max too. Kamran was supposed to get off work at eleven o'clock. He usually was home by 11:30. He would find out regardless, but Sean and I were worried how to tell Kamran. I left it up to Sean, and I knew Kamran would call me after he found out.

The phone rang at 11:30. Immediately after he said hi, Kamran asked if Sean was telling the truth about Max being missing. I tried to be strong for him and told him, "Don't worry, we are going to find Max."

"No, Mom, there is no way we will be able to find this dog," he said.

I asked why.

"Because somebody will have it by now. They eventually are going to find out what a good dog he is, and they probably know it's a very expensive dog. You think they are going to return it?" Kamran asked. Then he hung up.

I couldn't be on my legs anymore due to the stress I was under. I went to the bedroom and lay down. I had to hide my sorrow from my family as much as I could in order for them to stay strong. I stayed in bed until two o'clock, crying quietly and begging God for Max's safe return. I didn't want my husband to get more disturbed than he already was. I knew he wasn't himself, so I didn't want to make it worse for him. He loved Max too. Who didn't? He was a cute and sweet dog with good manners—and funny; I had never seen a dog as funny as Max. The more I thought about Max, the more I missed him.

The whole night I felt I was burning in a fever. I kept thinking, *Where is he? Is he in a safe place with good people? Is he cold and out there hiding somewhere? Is he hungry and thirsty? Is he with a bunch of kids who are torturing him?* My thoughts were killing me. My dad used to say, "My negative thoughts are my worst enemy, and my best friend is my positive and good thoughts." He was right: my negative thoughts were killing me. At some point I thought if he had died, at least I would know what had happened to him. But now I was going crazy because I knew he was alive and I didn't know where he was and what was going on with him. I fell asleep around three in the morning. I saw Max playing in the backyard. I woke up. It was around four, and I didn't even change my clothes. I had to drive to the kids' house very quickly before Max went away again. I was sure I would find him there.

Let me tell you first about the backyard at night. Since the backyard was very big with several corners and many trees (about twenty or more), lots of bushes, and a pool in the middle, it was beautiful during the day. But at night it was the scariest place I've ever seen. So I had never stepped in that backyard during the night before, especially since it wasn't attached to the house. The house was attached to a smaller backyard and then to the garage; at the other side of the garage was the backyard—that's the main reason I never felt safe there.

As soon as I got there, the first thing I checked was the back door, the door Max always waited at to come in. Unfortunately he wasn't there. Surprisingly I wasn't even thinking of the darkness of the backyard or it being unsafe and scary. I ran to the backyard and started to search it step-by-step. I kept calling Max's name. He wasn't there. I thought I might have missed some spots, so I took my time to look more carefully. I wasn't afraid of anything. The more I looked, the more disappointed I became. I collapsed on the grass and started to cry. I again asked God for Max's return.

After a while I headed to the car. Before I got in the car, I changed my mind. *He is in the backyard somewhere,* I thought. I went back to the yard and started to search one more time. There was a very dark tunnel attached to the pool that I had never been in, even during the day, due to its being so dark and scary. This time I went inside the tunnel from one side even though I couldn't see at all. I searched it by hand and came out the other side empty-handed. (Later on, when I thought about what I did that night, it scared the heck out of me.) I sat there for a minute and became mad at myself because due to my heavy schedule that day, I didn't stop by earlier to see him.

My regular schedule was I would stop by the kids' house around noon and spend some time with them. As soon as I went in, Max would shake my hand, and then I would take him for a walk. I also often took him for a ride, which he loved. I played with him in the backyard, then I would go to work, except for Tuesdays and Thursdays when I would stay longer. But as I said, that day I missed him because I had a lot to do. That's what really was bothering me.

When we have things, we don't appreciate or care that much. As soon as we lose them, we want them so desperately. If we are lucky enough to get another chance, we start to care. Isn't it better to appreciate and love what we have in the first place? I was going through so much plus feeling guilty on the side. I was asking God desperately for his safe return and to give me another chance.

I headed home disappointed. There was a church right across the street from where I live. Just before I got home, I turned into the church parking lot and sat in the car, praying and crying. I told God, "If Max is somewhere safe and having a good time, I am fine with it. But if he has a miserable life, please return him to us."

On June 3, my husband and I were ready to do more to find Max. The first thing we did, we headed to the kids' home, hoping Max might be by the door. He wasn't there. I searched the backyard again. I noticed the squirrels on the fence were waiting for him. They used to have so much fun chasing each other. Every corner I looked in reminded me how funny, well-behaved, and kind Max was. I had no control of my tears. Before I had left my house, I made sure to grab my dark glasses so nobody would see my tears or my red eyes.

I couldn't go in the kids' house because there was nobody waiting for me at the door to welcome me and shake my hand. The negative thoughts wouldn't leave me alone. *Is he still on the streets? Is he dead? Who got him? Is he hungry, thirsty, hurt, unhappy?* I started to search the neighborhood again. The more I searched the less result I got. Ali and I had prepared about two hundred flyers, but before we handed them out we called the animal shelter to find out if they had Max or any information about him. They didn't. We went around the neighborhood and started to put out the flyers. Each of us went a different way in order to do the job more quickly. We joined back up after two hours and decided to go other places together.

On the way we saw a lady outside in her front yard. Ali got out of the car and showed her Max's picture and asked, "Have you seen this dog?"

As soon as the lady saw the picture, she said that the preceding evening she had seen Max around Carlos O'Kelly's parking lot, being chased by two teenagers. I got out of the car very quickly after I heard she had some information about Max and asked her some more questions. We rushed to the restaurant and talked to the manager. Unfortunately they didn't have cameras in the parking lot. We put out lots of flyers and went back to the kids' house.

Ali called the *Wichita Eagle* to run an ad for a lost dog with all of Max's information. Kamran was in the shower, and Sean was adding his phone number to the flyers. When Kamran came downstairs, he was sad and his eyes were red; I realized he had been crying in the shower. I felt so heartbroken and decided to find Max at any cost. For two more hours we went around the city and put out the flyers, and then I had to go to work.

It was a hellish day for me at work. I usually have my smile on and make everybody laugh and make sure we have fun at work, but that day it was so difficult to do all these things. I felt like a dead person. Mostly I stayed downstairs trying to hide my red eyes. I was downstairs when I heard one of the employees calling my name, saying my husband was in the lobby waiting for me. I cleaned away my tears and went to him, hoping he had good news. As soon as I sat in front of him, I lost it and started to cry like a baby. At the same time my boss, who is a dog lover himself, walked in. He was nice enough to comfort me a little and made some useful suggestions. He also agreed that I could stick some flyers on the windows at work; I thought that was very nice of him.

I hadn't been able to eat anything since Max was gone. The stress inside me had melted all my energy. I tried to eat something, but I realized I couldn't swallow the food so I just stuck to drinking. My gut feeling was that Max was in a miserable situation, and there was no way I could think positively about his situation. Sean called me when the sun was going down to let me know he had put out all the flyers that he had. All of a sudden he lost it and started to cry on the phone. I told him not to worry. "We just need to keep praying and do our best to find him."

With flyers all over town, some more people called and said they had seen Max around Carlos O'Kelly's restaurant being chased by two teenagers. I got off work around eleven o'clock and started to search around again. Several times I thought I saw Max and got out of the car to look for him, but I guess it was only my imagination. Again before I got home, I stopped by the church and prayed more for Max's return. Almost the whole night I cried and prayed to God. My husband had copied about two hundred more flyers. We put them up all over town the next day. "The people who have him should see the flyers," I told Ali. Another night full of stress passed.

On June 4, very early in the morning, I headed to the kids' house again. I went straight to the back door to see if Max was waiting at the door, then I checked the backyard again, hoping he might be back. There was no sign of him. This time I went inside the house. It really broke my heart that he wasn't there anymore to welcome me at the door. I took several steps toward the living room and saw his water and food dishes with some food and water in them. My heart was squeezed so painfully in my chest.

I couldn't stand it there anymore. I ran to the backyard and cried like a baby again. I went back to our house. My husband was waiting for me with more flyers in his hand. We went back to the kids' house to ask if Sean was able to help us. Sean was the one who mostly took care of Max and bathed him and took him for his exercise. Sean and I got in one car and Ali in his car and went our separate ways. Every house where we took flyers, people kept saying it's difficult to find an expensive and fancy dog like Max, but for some reason I just couldn't let go.

The kids were going through the same pain as I was. Kamran loved this dog so much, and I knew he was very upset—that's why he was trying to hide from me. Most of our conversations took place on the phone; I kept calling and telling him not to worry. "I will find your dog, no matter what." I had to find the dog, mostly for Kamran's happiness.

"Mom, don't worry," he'd say. "We won't be able to find him. Just let go and go back to your normal life."

I said, "I am at my normal life; this is part of life."

"What are you doing now?" he asked.

"We are driving," I said.

"Where?" he asked.

"Around the neighborhood," I said.

"Look at your right side," he said.

I looked to the right, and he was there driving around the neighborhood too. "I decided to look around a little before I go to school," he said.

"I will find your dog, I promise," I said.

After several hours we all met at the shopping center. My husband's eyes were red. He said somebody had called his cell phone and told him she knew where Max was, but she needed to double-check and call Ali back in five minutes. It had already been an hour, and she hadn't called back yet. Bob suggested to Ali that he call her back instead. Ali did, but nobody answered the phone. Now we knew somebody knew something; otherwise they wouldn't call. We all went home and waited for more phone calls. Sean called the lady. This time she picked up the phone and said she was wrong, that wasn't our dog. Then she said, "That's an expensive dog. How much is the reward?"

"If you don't know where the dog is, why ask about the reward?" Sean asked, but the lady had hung up.

We all got so mad, confused, and hopeful. To me that was a light at the end of the tunnel. *That lady had the dog and was making sure we would give her a good reward, but why was she playing?* I thought. Ali and I went to put out more flyers, and Sean got on the computer to find that lady's address through her phone number.

When I got out of the car to put a flyer on a light pole, I saw a picture of a little missing girl there. It struck me so badly, I couldn't keep my tears from falling. It was a lost dog that I was looking for with all my energy; just imagine what that little girl's parents were going through. I said a prayer for them and her; I thought life would never be the same for her family and her.

Around five in the evening, Sean called and said he had found the lady's address. We rushed back home to get Sean to go to the address together. The third day of missing Max was coming to an end soon. We all sat in the living room very tired but hopeful. Suddenly the phone rang, and there was a gentleman on the other side.

"Did you lose a dog?" he asked.

"Yes," I said.

"When, where, what color, and what kind?"

I gave him all the information, and it matched with the dog they had found.

"I'll talk to my wife and call you back," he said and hung up.

My brain got so hot; I could feel the heat on my cheeks. I didn't know what to believe anymore. *Is somebody messing with me? Is he going to call back?* I asked myself. I looked at the caller ID; there was no phone number showing. I became so hot, confused, and dizzy. He called after two long minutes.

"My wife will bring Max where our kids found him three days ago," he said.

"Where did they find him?" I asked.

"By Carlos O'Kelly's," he said. "That's a very expensive dog."

"Yes, it is," I said.

"How much are you willing to give me?" he asked.

"Three hundred dollars," I said.

"Fine. My wife will see you there in ten minutes." He also gave me information about the car his wife was going to drive.

Ali said not to set my hopes too high. Something similar had happened to him earlier that day, and it really bothered him; he didn't want something like that to happen to me too.

"No, this is real, they have Max. Hurry up, let's go," I said. I called Bob and told him what had just happened; he said he would be there too. I didn't call Kamran, who was at work. I wanted to make sure I got Max, and then surprise him.

That was one of the longest rides of my life. I had mixed emotions. On the way I kept praying and hoping it was Max, not another dog. Finally we got there. I held up a big picture of Max and started to walk around the parking lot. My heart was pounding so badly I thought it might jump out of my chest any minute. It was fifteen minutes since the phone call; so far they were five minutes late.

My son's friend said, "They might be messing with you."

I said, "No, the way the gentleman was talking, he had Max."

All of a sudden a car pulled in with the description the gentleman had given me. They drove toward me but they passed me. They circled around and came back toward me, stopping right in front of me. I kept looking inside the car but couldn't see Max. A lady jumped out of the car and said she had the dog. I quickly looked inside the car again but still didn't see any dog. I looked at the lady again, but before I could say anything, she opened the back door and I saw Max squeezed down on the floor.

I looked at him again and couldn't believe my eyes. He looked so miserable, weak, and dirty. I grabbed him in my arms and sat on the ground, crying from the bottom of my heart. My husband held him for a moment with tears coming down from his eyes. Sean and Bob did the same thing. The lady said she tried to feed Max but he hadn't been eating—that's why he couldn't walk or even hold his head straight. I thanked her and paid the three hundred dollars.

We rushed to the kids' house and brought Max his own water dish. He started to drink. I had never seen him that thirsty; he drank for almost three minutes. He started to walk a little. I suggested that Sean give him a bath and then feed him. Ali and I went home. On the way home, I asked Ali to stop by the church to thank God. I couldn't believe my prayers had been answered once more.

The next thing I did was to call Kamran and give him the good news. He picked up the phone, sounding so tired.

"Kamran, I have good news for you. Remember I said I would find your dog no matter what? Well, we found him," I said. No feeling is better than that of a mother who makes her children happy. I couldn't believe how the tone of his voice changed. A minute ago he sounded like the most tired son. All of a sudden after hearing the good news, he sounded like the happiest son.

"Thank you, thank you, Mom. You are the best. Bye," he said.

The first thing Bob did the next day was to take him to the vet for a checkup. Everything was fine. For almost two days Max wasn't himself. After that he gained his energy and went back to his normal life. Everybody else did too. The only difference was that everybody was paying more attention to Max.

Without lows and highs, life has no meaning.

SOME OF MY LEARNINGS IN LIFE

I learned plenty of valuable life lessons while living in America and Iran.

I learned that if everything I do, I do by saying God's name, I will get a better result.

I learned that helping others is a free therapy to lift my spirit.

I learned that the best possible way to be happy is to do everything in God's way.

I learned that the best attachment we can have is the one we have toward God, because we never lose him; he is the only one that exists forever.

I learned that the worst thing in life is attachment; it hurts badly when we lose it.

I learned to have a huge respect for the people who remain true behind my back, not the people who act true to my face.

I learned the three most valuable lessons of my life: respect for self, respect for others, and taking responsibility for all my actions.

I learned to admit my mistake and take immediate action to fix it.

I learned I should spend some time alone every day.

I learned a true relationship is not a relationship in good times, but is one that is true in critical situations.

I learned that difficult experiences bring out the best abilities in us.

I learned I need to work on the power inside me to get rid of the fear inside me.

I learned that love changes people.

I learned that when you have a dream, trust it and go for it completely without any doubt. At the end you will either experience a life lesson or achieve success.

I learned as I got older, in order to look back and enjoy the moments that I have already been in, I should live a good and honorable life.

I learned that in disagreements with friends and loved ones, never bring up the past.

I learned I should share my knowledge and learn the knowledge of others.

I learned that instead of judging the mistakes of others, I should recognize mine.

I learned not to make any decisions when I am angry.

I learned not to pay for a job until it is finished.

I learned sometimes all a person needs is a hug.

I learned to be gentle with the earth, to love, respect, and enjoy nature.

I learned, in order to get, I need to give.

I learned to stay away from those who have nothing to lose.

I learned that it is good to be important, but being good is more important.

I learned that living in the past is like chasing clouds.

I learned I should welcome great risks if I hope for great achievement in life.

I learned to never damage a relationship by a little dispute.

I learned how to say *no* with kindness.

I learned to take away something from everything that I spend my life and my time on.

I learned to love and care for my loved ones as if it's the last day of their lives.

I learned that my trash might be somebody else's treasure.

I learned not to put things off; do it now.

I learned to have an easy, honest, and natural relationship with others.

I learned it's important what I say, but it's more important how I say it.

I learned that lives can be destroyed easily because of lack of knowledge.

I learned that sometimes the things that we think are working against us are the things that work out for us.

I learned that in order to get help from others, I should take the first step.

I learned that in order to love and take care of my loved ones, I should work on having a beautiful mind, a healthy body, and good spirit.

I learned in order to follow the truth, I should tell myself the truth.

I learned not to be so hard on myself and to be more flexible.

I learned to be careful and thoughtful about the words that come out of my mouth.

I learned, in order to have an easy and stress-free life, I should do things in a right way.

I learned to care for, love, help, and respect my loved ones when they are alive and need it.

I learned that no amount of money will buy a failed reputation.

I learned the best wealth is health.

I learned to look for somebody who can turn a sad day to a joyful day for me.

I learned that the most beautiful things on this earth are free for both the poor and the rich: a beautiful relaxing blue sky, a magnificent sunrise and sunset, gifted colorful flowers and greens, the blue ocean, and a whole lot more.

I learned God exists but we don't see him; the blue color of the sky and the sea doesn't exist but we see it.

I learned that under some serious and grumpy faces there are wonderful hearts; never judge a book by its cover.

I learned that I should do the right thing regardless of what people think of me.

I learned that in order for others to think positively about me, I must think positively about myself.

I learned that when we plan to get revenge against someone, we are only digging a hole for ourselves to fall in; we are letting that person continue to hurt us more.

I learned not to be afraid or ashamed to say, "I don't know," when I don't.

I learned that the best way to live, grow, and learn is to surround myself with people smarter than me and with useful books.

I learned that grief about the past and fear of the future kill the enjoyment of the present.

I learned that in order to have a beautiful and free spirit, I must get closer to God, worship him more, and follow his laws.

I learned that God is in the smile that we put on a needy person's face.

I learned to be aware of the art of listening.

I learned I shouldn't give up my valuable values under any circumstances.

I learned it's never too late to become a better person.

I learned that a smile is the most powerful and best way to greet someone we meet.

I learned that nothing ever stays the same in life.

I learned I don't need other people to be able to love myself.

I learned that sometimes silence is a better solution to calm an angry person down.

I learned that to ignore the truth and realities won't change the facts about the truth and realities.

I learned I can't rely on others to solve my problems.

I learned to always tell the truth.

I learned to think, love, care, pay attention, and enjoy the things that I have, not be sad about the things that I don't have.

I learned that if I love what I'm doing, I do it from the bottom of my heart and right.

I learned that I wish I could have told my grandparents how much I loved them before they passed away.

I learned that sometimes animals can make a man happier than a person can.

I learned that love is not only an emotion but also a need.

I learned that when a door closes in our life, another door opens—but sometimes we are so busy focusing on the closed door that we don't see the open one.

I learned that being a good person doesn't cost anything. As I said earlier, the best things are free on this earth for both the poor and the rich.

I learned that nobody in life will get what they thought they would get.

I learned that I can't buy a good friend; I need to find one.

I learned that love is a peaceful treasure and peace is a valuable one.

I learned that it's never too late to learn, to forgive, and to forget.

I learned that fear kills my confidence; when there is no confidence, there is no me.

I learned that in order to have a better relationship with others, I should have a flexible personality and be easygoing.

I learned that sometimes the breakups are the blessings.

I learned to breathe deeply several times a day; it relaxes me in many ways.

I learned there are some angels without wings who live on this earth.

I learned that gaining things is success; enjoying things is happiness.

I learned that the best way to achieve success is to keep trying.

I learned that if there is such a thing as bad or good in our life, it's all about our choices.

I learned that being addicted to smiling, loving, forgiving, forgetting, and sharing are the best addictions.

I learned that if I think I can do something and I put my mind, my energy, and my time into it, I succeed.

I learned that the most beautiful things are not visible but are the true love and feelings from the heart.

I learned that self-confidence is the most important step toward success.

I learned that trust, respect, and being responsible are the most important factors in having a good relationship.

I learned that I should seek happiness in my mind and heart, nowhere else.

I learned that kindness never dies.

I learned that I should be a reason for one's happiness, not a part of one's happiness. I should be a part of someone's grief, not the reason for one's grief.

I learned that I am made of my choices, my decisions, my thoughts, and my beliefs.

I learned that drops of rain aren't alive, yet they give life to all humans, animals, trees, and flowers; they bring everything to life.

I learned that in order to have a peaceful mind and life, I should like my enemies too.

I learned that I will always live in the past if I don't pursue learning to achieve a better life.

I learned that if I do good, good comes to me.

I learned that to have social power, I need to have a positive attitude.

I learned that breaking my promises is like breaking myself.

I learned that the happiness of my life depends on the quality of my thought.

I learned that ideas won't work unless you give them a try.

I learned we can't achieve happiness without being spiritual.

I learned I should accept trouble from God just as I accept good things.

I learned that sometimes the smallest amount can have the biggest impact on children's lives.

I learned two days I shouldn't worry about: yesterday and tomorrow.

I learned that if I fail an attempt, I should never fail to make another one.

I learned that wisdom comes with knowledge, age, and experience and needs to be respected.

I learned that thinking positive brings out unknown abilities in you.

I learned that one of the secrets to success is to forget about the past.

I learned that if I love and respect myself, I'll be able to make others love and respect me too.

I learned that almost all the time, losing leads to winning.

I learned that the best way possible to use my eyes is to look at beautiful things.

I learned that the best way possible to use my ears is to listen to beautiful things.

I learned that to get the best use of my legs, I must go to beautiful places.

I learned that to get the best use of my heart, I must feel the most beautiful things.

I learned that to get the best use of my mind, I must dump the most beautiful things into it.

I learned that the best possible way to use my hands is to give away with warm hands.

I learned to exercise and eat right before I gain weight.

I learned to have love toward God's creatures and animals.

I learned there are lots of things I still need to learn.

MY FINAL THOUGHTS

I think America is and can be a perfect dreamland for those who use freedom in the right way. I think America is the land of liberty and human rights, where innocent human lives are protected. I think most Americans look to the government to solve all the problems that I mentioned in this book, not realizing that they as parents are the key to helping solve most of these problems.

I think if schools and parents maintain strong relationships and unity between them, a lot of problems will easily be solved. Parents are the key. Let's work together to make this country greater than ever. Each individual needs to speak up. We can't lay all the problems on others' shoulders to get solved. If we as individuals don't help share in fixing these problems, every single person is going to get hurt—first our children and parents, then society, then the country, and then the earth. And of course, there is not going to be a wonderful future for America if we as parents ignore the problems. Most problems start from family, from our house.

Good luck!

ABOUT THE AUTHOR

Mahnaz B. Consolver, also the author of *The Darkest Days of My Life in the U.S. and Iran*, was born and raised in Iran. She moved to the United States for the first time in 1979 with her first husband, but then moved back to Iran in 1982 with their first little boy. In 1996 she and her three sons moved back to the United States, where she remarried. She currently lives with her husband and dog in Kansas.